With Cram101.com online, you also have access to extensive reference material.

You will nail those essays and papers. Here is an example from a Cram101 Biology text:

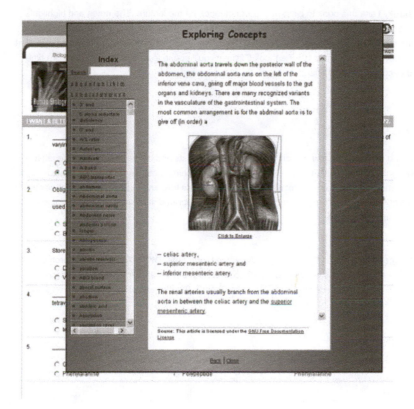

Visit **www.Cram101.com**, click Sign Up at the top of the screen, and enter DK73DW9457 in the promo code box on the registration screen. Access to www.Cram101.com is normally $9.95 per month, but because you have purchased this book, your access fee is only $4.95 per month, cancel at any time. Sign up and stop highlighting textbooks forever.

Learning System

Cram101 Textbook Outlines is a learning system. The notes in this book are the highlights of your textbook, you will never have to highlight a book again.

How to use this book. Take this book to class, it is your notebook for the lecture. The notes and highlights on the left hand side of the pages follow the outline and order of the textbook. All you have to do is follow along while your instructor presents the lecture. Circle the items emphasized in class and add other important information on the right side. With Cram101 Textbook Outlines you'll spend less time writing and more time listening. Learning becomes more efficient.

Cram101.com Online

Increase your studying efficiency by using Cram101.com's practice tests and online reference material. It is the perfect complement to Cram101 Textbook Outlines. Use self-teaching matching tests or simulate in-class testing with comprehensive multiple choice tests, or simply use Cram's true and false tests for quick review. Cram101.com even allows you to enter your in-class notes for an integrated studying format combining the textbook notes with your class notes.

Visit **www.Cram101.com**, click Sign Up at the top of the screen, and enter **DK73DW9457** in the promo code box on the registration screen. Access to www.Cram101.com is normally $9.95 per month, but because you have purchased this book, your access fee is only $4.95 per month. Sign up and stop highlighting textbooks forever.

Cram101 Textbook Outlines to accompany:

Development Economics

Debraj Ray, 1st Edition

A Cram101 Inc. publication (c) 2010.

PRACTICE EXAMS.

Get all of the self-teaching practice exams for each chapter of this textbook at **www.Cram101.com** and ace the tests. Here is an example:

Chapter 1

Development Economics
Debraj Ray, 1st Edition,
All Material Written and Prepared by Cram101

I WANT A BETTER GRADE.   Items 1 - 50 of 100.

1 _____ is a term generally used to describe a nation with a low level of material well being. There is no single internationally-recognized definition of developed country, and the levels of development may vary widely within so-called developing countries, with some developing countries having high average standards of living.

Some international organizations like the World Bank use strictly numerical classifications.

- ⦾ Developing country
- ⦾ Daily News
- ⦾ Dahrendorf hypothesis
- ⦾ Dalton Trail

2 The term _____ arose during the Cold War to define countries that remained non-aligned or neutral with either capitalism and NATO (which along with its allies represented the First World) or communism and the Soviet Union (which along with its allies represented the Second World). This definition provided a way of broadly categorizing the nations of the Earth into three groups based on social, political, and economic divisions. Although the term continues to be used colloquially to describe the poorest countries in the world, this usage is widely disparaged since the term no longer holds any verifiable meaning after the fall of the Soviet Union deprecated the terms First World and Second World.

- ⦾ Third World
- ⦾ Tail risk
- ⦾ Taguchi loss function
- ⦾ Tail value at risk

3 In economics, _____ (TFP) is a variable which accounts for effects in total output not

You get a 50% discount for the online exams. Go to **Cram101.com**, click Sign Up at the top of the screen, and enter DK73DW9457 in the promo code box on the registration screen. Access to Cram101.com is $4.95 per month, cancel at any time.

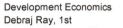

Development Economics
Debraj Ray, 1st

CONTENTS

Developing country	Developing country is a term generally used to describe a nation with a low level of material well being. There is no single internationally-recognized definition of developed country, and the levels of development may vary widely within so-called developing countries, with some developing countries having high average standards of living.
	Some international organizations like the World Bank use strictly numerical classifications.
Third World	The term Third World arose during the Cold War to define countries that remained non-aligned or neutral with either capitalism and NATO (which along with its allies represented the First World) or communism and the Soviet Union (which along with its allies represented the Second World). This definition provided a way of broadly categorizing the nations of the Earth into three groups based on social, political, and economic divisions. Although the term continues to be used colloquially to describe the poorest countries in the world, this usage is widely disparaged since the term no longer holds any verifiable meaning after the fall of the Soviet Union deprecated the terms First World and Second World.
Total-factor productivity	In economics, total-factor productivity (TFP) is a variable which accounts for effects in total output not caused by inputs. For example, a year with unusually good weather will tend to have higher output, because bad weather hinders agricultural output. A variable like weather does not directly relate to unit inputs, so weather is considered a total-factor productivity variable.
Underdevelopment	Underdevelopment is the state of an organization (e.g. a country) that has not reached its maturity. Most Sub-Saharan African countries remain largely underdeveloped - street in Dakar, Senegal.
	It is often used to refer to economic Underdevelopment, symptoms of which include lack of access to job opportunities, health care, drinkable water, food, education and housing.
	Underdevelopment takes place when resources are not used to their full socio-economic potential, with the result that local or regional development is slower in most cases than it should be.
Factor	A factor or limiting resource is a factor that controls a process, such as organism growth or species population, size, or distribution. The availability of food, predation pressure, or availability of shelter are examples of factors that could be limiting for an organism. An example of a limiting factor is sunlight, which is crucial in rainforests.
Information	Information as a concept has many meanings, from everyday usage to technical settings. The concept of Information is closely related to notions of constraint, communication, control, data, form, instruction, knowledge, meaning, mental stimulus, pattern, perception, and representation.
	The English word was apparently derived from the Latin accusative form of the nominative (informatio): this noun is in its turn derived from the verb "informare" (to inform) in the sense of "to give form to the mind", "to discipline", "instruct", "teach": "Men so wise should go and inform their kings." (1330) Inform itself comes from the Latin verb informare, to give form to, to form an idea of.
Missing Market	A Missing market is a situation in microeconomics where a competitive market allowing the exchange of a commodity would be Pareto-efficient, but no such market exists.
	A variety of factors can lead to Missing markets:
	A classic example of a Missing market is the case of an externality like pollution, where decision makers are not responsible for some of the consequences of their actions. When a factory discharges polluted water into a river, that pollution can hurt people who fish in or get their drinking water from the river downstream, but the factory owner may have no incentive to consider those consequences.

Anecdotal value	In economics, Anecdotal value refers to the primarily social and political value of an anecdote or anecdotal evidence in promoting understanding of a social, cultural, in the last several decades the evaluation of anecdotes has received sustained academic scrutiny from economists and scholars such as S.G. Checkland (on David Ricardo), Steven Novella, Hollis Robbins, R. Charleton, Kwamena Kwansah-Aidoo, and others; these academics seek to quantify the value inherent in the deployment of anecdotes. More recently, economists studying choice models have begun assessing Anecdotal value in the context of framing; Kahneman and Tversky suggest that choice models may be contingent on stories or anecdotes that frame or influence choice.
Gross national product	A variety of measures of national income and output are used in economics to estimate total economic activity in a country or region, including gross domestic product (GDP), Gross National Product , and net national income (NNI).
	There are three main ways of calculating these numbers; the output approach, the income approach and the expenditure approach. In theory, the three must yield the same, because total expenditures on goods and services must equal the total income paid to the producers (GNI), and that must also equal the total value of the output of goods and services .
Exchange rate	Exchange rates Currency band Exchange rate Exchange rate regime Fixed Exchange rate Floating Exchange rate Linked Exchange rate
	Markets effective Exchange rate · 5 Uncovered interest rate parity · 6 Asset market model · 7 Fluctuations in Exchange rates · 8 .
Income distribution	In economics, the Lorenz curve is a graphical representation of the cumulative distribution function of a probability distribution; it is a graph showing the proportion of the distribution assumed by the bottom y% of the values. It is often used to represent income Distribution, where it shows for the bottom x% of households, what percentage y% of the total income they have. The percentage of households is plotted on the x-axis, the percentage of income on the y-axis.
Per capita Income	per capita income means how much each individual receives, in monetary terms, of the yearly income generated in the country. This is what each citizen is to receive if the yearly national income is divided equally among everyone. per capita income is usually reported in units of currency per year.
Good	In macroeconomics and accounting, a good is contrasted with a service. In this sense, a good is defined as a physical (tangible) product, capable of being delivered to a purchaser and involves the transfer of ownership from seller to customer, say an apple, as opposed to an (intangible) service, say a haircut. A more general term that preserves the distinction between goods and services is "commodities," like a flashlight.

Price	price in economics and business is the result of an exchange and from that trade we assign a numerical monetary value to a good, service or asset. If Alice trades Bob 4 apples for an orange, the price of an orange is 4 apples. Inversely, the price of an apple is 1/4 oranges.
Production	Production refers to the economic process of converting of inputs into outputs and is a field of study in microeconomics. Production uses resources to create a good or service that is suitable for exchange. This can include manufacturing, storing, shipping, and packaging.
Purchasing Power Parity	The Purchasing power parity theory uses the long-term equilibrium exchange rate of two currencies to equalize their purchasing power. Developed by Gustav Cassel in 1918, it is based on the law of one price: the theory states that, in ideally efficient markets, identical goods should have only one price. This purchasing power SEM rate equalizes the purchasing power of different currencies in their home countries for a given basket of goods.
Interest	In the Renaissance era, greater mobility of people facilitated an increase in commerce and the appearance of appropriate conditions for entrepreneurs to start new, lucrative businesses. Given that borrowed money was no longer strictly for consumption but for production as well, Interest was no longer viewed in the same manner. The School of Salamanca elaborated on various reasons that justified the charging of Interest: the person who received a loan benefited, and one could consider Interest as a premium paid for the risk taken by the loaning party.
Distortion	A Distortion is the alteration of the original shape (or other characteristic) of an object, image, sound, waveform or other form of information or representation. Distortion is usually unwanted. In some fields, Distortion is desirable, such as electric guitar (where Distortion is often induced purposely with the amplifier or an electronic effect to achieve an aggressive sound where desired).
Doubling time	The Doubling time is the period of time required for a quantity to double in size or value. It is applied to population growth, inflation, resource extraction, consumption of goods, compound interest, the volume of malignant tumours, and many other things which tend to grow over time. When the relative growth rate (not the absolute growth rate) is constant, the quantity undergoes exponential growth and has a constant Doubling time or period which can be calculated directly from the growth rate.
Economic expansion	An Economic expansion is an increase in the level of economic activity, and of the goods and services available in the market place. Its is a period of economic growth as measured by a rise in real GDP. Typically it relates to an upturn in production and utilization of resources. Economic recovery and prosperity are two successive phases of expansion.
Change	changes can refer to: · A jazz term for chord progression · changes (band), an American folk band · The changes (band), an American rock band

· changes (The Monkees album), The Monkees" ninth studio album
· changes, Christopher Wiliams" second studio album
· changes, an album by R. Carlos Nakai
· changes (Taylor Horn album), Taylor Horn"s third studio album
· changesbowie, a David Bowie compilation album
· changes (Kelly Osbourne album), Kelly Osbourne"s second studio album
· changes (Vanilla Sky album), Vanilla Sky"s third album
· changes (Jarrett album), by Keith Jarrett, Jack DeJohnette and Gary Peacock
· changes (Billy "Crash" Craddock album)
· changes (Lisa Miskovsky album)
· changes (Tanya Tucker album)
· changes, an album by Johnny Rivers

· "changes" (David Bowie song), a song by David Bowie on his 1971 album Hunky Dory
· "changes" (2Pac song), a song by Tupac Shakur on his Greatest Hits album
· "changes" (Black Sabbath song), a ballad by Black Sabbath, remade as a duet by Kelly and Ozzy Osbourne
· "changes" (Will Young song), a song by Will Young on his fourth studio album, Let It Go
· "changes" (Gareth Gates song), a song by Gareth Gates, from the album Pictures of the Other Side
· "changes" (Imagination song), a song by Imagination, from the album In the Heat of the Night
· "changes", a song by Yes on the album 90125
· "changes", a song by "Buddy" Miles ' Jimi Hendrix on the album Band of Gypsys
· "changes", a song by Jane"s Addiction
· "changes", a song by Phil Ochs
· "changes", a song by Godsmack on the album Faceless
· "changes", a song by The Zombies on the album Odessey and Oracle
· "changes", a song by 3 Doors Down on the album Away from the Sun
· "changes", a song by Sugar on the album Copper Blue
· "changes", a song by Chris Lake
· "changes", a song by Moby Grape on their album Moby Grape
· "changes", a song by Santana on their album Zebop!

· The changes (TV series), produced by the BBC in 1975. Also the changes Trilogy of novels on which the series was based, written by Peter Dickinson .

Standard of living	Standard of living is generally measured by standards such as real (i.e. inflation adjusted) income per person and poverty rate. Other measures such as access and quality of health care, income growth inequality and educational standards are also used. Examples are access to certain goods (such as number of refrigerators per 1000 people), or measures of health such as life expectancy.
Share	In financial markets, a Share is a unit of account for various financial instruments including stocks (ordinary or preferential), and investments in limited partnerships, and REITs. The common feature of all these is equity participation (limited in the case of preference Shares).

	In American English, the plural stocks is widely used instead of Shares, in other words to refer to the stock (or perhaps originally stock certificates) of even a single company.
Inequality	In mathematics, an inequality is a statement about the relative size or order of two objects
Economic Growth	Economic growth is an increase in activity in an economy. It is often measured as the rate of change of gross domestic product (GDP). Economic growth refers only to the quantity of goods and services produced; it says nothing about the way in which they are produced.
Life expectancy	Life expectancy is the expected (in the statistical sense) number of years of life remaining at a given age. It is denoted by e_x, which means the average number of subsequent years of life for someone now aged x, according to a particular mortality experience. (In technical literature, this symbol means the average number of complete years of life remaining, ie excluding fractions of a year.
Disease	A Disease or medical condition is an abnormal condition of an organism that impairs bodily functions, associated with specific symptoms and signs. It may be caused by external factors, such as invading organisms, or it may be caused by internal dysfunctions, such as autoimmune Diseases.
	In human beings, "Disease" is often used more broadly to refer to any condition that causes pain, dysfunction, distress, social problems, and/or death to the person afflicted, or similar problems for those in contact with the person.
Literacy	Literacy is a concept claimed and defined by a range of different theoretical fields. In everyday terms, "Literacy" is typically described as the ability to read and write. The United Nations Educational, Scientific and Cultural Organization (UNESCO) has drafted a definition of Literacy as the "ability to identify, understand, interpret, create, communicate, compute and use printed and written materials associated with varying contexts.
Human development index	The human development index is an index used to rank countries by level of "human development", which usually also implies whether a country is developed, developing, or underdeveloped.
	The human development index combines normalized measures of life expectancy, educational attainment, and GDP per capita for countries worldwide. It is claimed as a standard means of measuring human development--a concept that, according to the United Nations Development Program (UNDP), refers to the process of widening the options of persons, giving them greater opportunities for education, health care, income, employment, etc.
Quality of life	
	Two widely known measures of a country"s liveability are the Economist Intelligence Unit"s Quality of life index and the Mercer Quality of Living Survey. Both measures calculate the liveability of countries around the world through a combination of subjective life-satisfaction surveys and objective determinants of Quality of life such as divorce rates, safety, and infrastructure. Such measures relate more broadly to the population of a city, state, or country, not to the individual level.
Scatter plot	A scatter plot is a type of mathematical diagram using Cartesian coordinates to display values for two variables for a set of data.

The data is displayed as a collection of points, each having the value of one variable determining the position on the horizontal axis and the value of the other variable determining the position on the vertical axis. A scatter plot is also called a scatter chart, scatter diagram and scatter graph.

Birth rate

Crude Birth rate is the nativity or childbirths per 1,000 people per year.

According to the United Nations" World Population Prospects: The 2008 Revision Population Database, crude Birth rate is the Number of births over a given period divided by the person-years lived by the population over that period. It is expressed as number of births per 1,000 population.

Informal sector

The Informal sector is economic activity that is neither taxed nor monitored by a government; and is not included in that government"s Gross National Product (GNP); as opposed to a formal economy.

Although the informal economy is often associated with developing countries --where up to 60% of the labor force (with as much 40% of GDP) works, all economic systems contain an informal economy in some proportion. The term "Informal sector" was used in many earlier studies, and has been mostly replaced in more recent studies which use the newer term.

Trade

Trade is the voluntary exchange of goods, services, or both. Trade is also called commerce or transaction. A mechanism that allows Trade is called a market.

International Trade

International trade is exchange of capital, goods, and services across international borders or territories. In most countries, it represents a significant share of gross domestic product (GDP). While International trade has been present throughout much of history , its economic, social, and political importance has been on the rise in recent centuries.

Primary Products

The primary sector of the economy involves changing natural resources into Primary products. Most products from this sector are considered raw materials for other industries. Major businesses in this sector include agriculture, agribusiness, fishing, forestry and all mining and quarrying industries.

Consumer

Consumer is a broad label that refers to any individuals or households that use goods and services generated within the economy. The concept of a Consumer is used in different contexts, so that the usage and significance of the term may vary.

Typically when business people and economists talk of Consumers they are talking about person as Consumer, an aggregated commodity item with little individuality other than that expressed in the buy/not-buy decision.

Terms of trade

In international economics and international trade, terms of trade is the relative prices of a country"s export to import. "terms of trade" are sometimes used as a proxy for the relative social welfare of a country, but this heuristic is technically questionable and should be used with extreme caution. An improvement in a nation"s terms of trade (the increase of the ratio) is good for that country in the sense that it has to pay less for the products it imports.

Import

Balance of trade represents a difference in value f and export for a country. A country has demand for an Import when domestic quantity demanded exceeds domestic quantity supplied, or when the price of the good (or service) on the world market is less than the price on the domestic market.

The balance of trade, usually denoted NX, is the difference between the value of the goods (and services) a country exports and the value of the goods the country Imports:

NX = X − I, or equivalently I = X − NX

A trade deficit occurs when Imports are large relative to exports.

Anecdotal value	In economics, Anecdotal value refers to the primarily social and political value of an anecdote or anecdotal evidence in promoting understanding of a social, cultural, in the last several decades the evaluation of anecdotes has received sustained academic scrutiny from economists and scholars such as S.G. Checkland (on David Ricardo), Steven Novella, Hollis Robbins, R. Charleton, Kwamena Kwansah-Aidoo, and others; these academics seek to quantify the value inherent in the deployment of anecdotes. More recently, economists studying choice models have begun assessing Anecdotal value in the context of framing; Kahneman and Tversky suggest that choice models may be contingent on stories or anecdotes that frame or influence choice.
Economic Growth	Economic growth is an increase in activity in an economy. It is often measured as the rate of change of gross domestic product (GDP). Economic growth refers only to the quantity of goods and services produced; it says nothing about the way in which they are produced.
Cooperation	Distinguish from Corporation. Cooperation, co-operation, or coöperation is the process of working or acting together, which can be accomplished by both intentional and non-intentional agents. In its simplest form it involves things working in harmony, side by side, while in its more complicated forms, it can involve something as complex as the inner workings of a human being or even the social patterns of a nation.
Per capita Income	per capita income means how much each individual receives, in monetary terms, of the yearly income generated in the country. This is what each citizen is to receive if the yearly national income is divided equally among everyone. per capita income is usually reported in units of currency per year.
Final good	In economics final goods are goods that are ultimately consumed rather than used in the production of another good. For example, a car sold to a consumer is a final good; the components such as tires sold to the car manufacturer are not; they are intermediate goods used to make the final good. When used in measures of national income and output the term final goods only includes new goods.
Good	In macroeconomics and accounting, a good is contrasted with a service. In this sense, a good is defined as a physical (tangible) product, capable of being delivered to a purchaser and involves the transfer of ownership from seller to customer, say an apple, as opposed to an (intangible) service, say a haircut. A more general term that preserves the distinction between goods and services is "commodities," like a flashlight.
Demand	In economics, demand is the desire to own anything and the ability to pay for it. . The term demand signifies the ability or the willingness to buy a particular commodity at a given point of time.
Gross national product	A variety of measures of national income and output are used in economics to estimate total economic activity in a country or region, including gross domestic product (GDP), Gross National Product , and net national income (NNI). There are three main ways of calculating these numbers; the output approach, the income approach and the expenditure approach. In theory, the three must yield the same, because total expenditures on goods and services must equal the total income paid to the producers (GNI), and that must also equal the total value of the output of goods and services .

Distribution	Distribution in economics refers to the way total output or income is distributed among individuals or among the factors of production (labor, land, and capital) (Samuelson and Nordhaus, 2001, p. 762). In general theory and the national income and product accounts, each unit of output corresponds to a unit of income. One use of national accounts is for classifying factor incomes and measuring their respective shares, as in National Income.
Dot-com bubble	The "Dot-com bubble" (or) was a speculative bubble covering roughly 1998-2001 (with a climax on March 10, 2000 with the NASDAQ peaking at 5132.52) during which stock markets in Western nations saw their equity value rise rapidly from growth in the more recent Internet sector and related fields. While the latter part was a boom and bust cycle, the Internet boom sometimes is meant to refer to the steady commercial growth of the Internet with the advent of the world wide web as exemplified by the first release of the Mosaic web browser in 1993 and continuing through the 1990s.
	The period was marked by the founding (and, in many cases, spectacular failure) of a group of new Internet-based companies commonly referred to as dot-coms.
Time horizon	A Time horizon, also known as a planning horizon, is a fixed point of time in the future at which point certain processes will be evaluated or assumed to end. It is necessary in an accounting, finance or risk management regime to assign such a fixed horizon time so that alternatives can be evaluated for performance over the same period of time. A Time horizon is a physical impossibility in the real world.
Endogeneity	In an economic model, a parameter or variable are said to be endogenous when there is a correlation between the parameter or variable and the error term. Endogeneity can arise as a result of measurement error, autoregression with autocorrelated errors, simultaneity, omitted variables, and sample selection errors (Kennedy p 139).
	For example, in a simple supply and demand model, when predicting the quantity demanded in equilibrium, the price is endogenous because producers change their price in response to demand and consumers change their demand in response to price.
Capital accumulation	Most generally, the accumulation of capital refers simply to the gathering or amassment of objects of value; the increase in wealth; or the creation of wealth. Capital can be generally defined as assets invested with the expectation that their value will increase, usually because there is the expectation of profit, rent, interest, royalties, capital gain or some other kind of return.
	The definition of Capital accumulation is subject to controversy and ambiguities, because it could refer to a net addition to existing wealth, or to a redistribution of wealth.
Birth rate	Crude Birth rate is the nativity or childbirths per 1,000 people per year.
	According to the United Nations" World Population Prospects: The 2008 Revision Population Database, crude Birth rate is the Number of births over a given period divided by the person-years lived by the population over that period. It is expressed as number of births per 1,000 population.
Demographic	Demographics data refers to selected population characteristics as used in government, marketing or opinion research). Commonly-used Demographics include race, age, income, disabilities, mobility (in terms of travel time to work or number of vehicles available), educational attainment, home ownership, employment status, and even location.

Demographic transition	The Demographic transition model (DTM) is a model used to represent the process of explaining the transformation of countries from high birth rates and high death rates to low birth rates and low death rates as part of the economic development of a country from a pre-industrial to an industrialized economy. It is based on an interpretation begun in 1929 by the American demographer Warren Thompson of prior observed changes, or transitions, in birth and death rates in industrialized societies over the past two hundred years.
	Most developed countries are beyond stage three of the model; the majority of developing countries are in stage 2 or stage 3. The model was based on the changes seen in Europe so these countries follow the DTM relatively well.
Production	Production refers to the economic process of converting of inputs into outputs and is a field of study in microeconomics. Production uses resources to create a good or service that is suitable for exchange. This can include manufacturing, storing, shipping, and packaging.
Production function	In economics, a Production function is a function that specifies the output of a firm, an industry) compares the practice of the existing entities converting inputs X into output y to determine the most efficient practice Production function of the existing entities, whether the most efficient feasible practice production or the most efficient actual practice production. In either case, the maximum output of a technologically-determined production process is a mathematical function of input factors of production.
Steady state	A system in a Steady state has numerous properties that are unchanging in time. The concept of Steady state has relevance in many fields, in particular thermodynamics. Steady state is a more general situation than dynamic equilibrium.
Diminishing returns	In economics, Diminishing returns refers to how the marginal production of a factor of production, in contrast to the increase that would otherwise be normally expected, actually starts to progressively decrease the more of the factor are added. According to this relationship, in a production system with fixed and variable inputs (say factory size and labor), beyond some point, each additional unit of the variable input (IE man*hours) yields smaller and smaller increases in outputs, also reducing the mean productivity of each worker. Conversely, producing one more unit of output, costs more and more (due to the major amount of variable inputs being used, to little effect)
	This concept is also known as the law of diminishing marginal returns or the law of increasing relative cost.
Productivity	Productivity is a measure of output from a production process, per unit of input. For example, lab is typically measured as a ratio of output per labor-hour, an input. Productivity may be conceived of as a metric of the technical or engineering efficiency of production.
Alternative hypothesis	In statistical hypothesis testing, the Alternative hypothesis (or maintained hypothesis or research hypothesis) and the null hypothesis are the two rival hypotheses which are compared by a statistical hypothesis test. An example might be where water quality in a stream has been observed over many years and a test is made of the null hypothesis that there is no change in quality between the first and second halves of the data against the Alternative hypothesis that the quality is poorer in the second half of the record.
	The concept of an Alternative hypothesis in testing was devised by Jerzy Neyman and Egon Pearson, and it is used in the Neyman-Pearson lemma.

Hypothesis testing	A statistical hypothesis test is a method of making statistical decisions using experimental data. In statistics, a result is called statistically significant if it is unlikely to have occurred by chance. The phrase "test of significance" was coined by Ronald Fisher: "Critical tests of this kind may be called tests of significance, and when such tests are available we may discover whether a second sample is or is not significantly different from the first."

hypothesis testing is sometimes called confirmatory data analysis, in contrast to exploratory data analysis. |
| Trade | Trade is the voluntary exchange of goods, services, or both. Trade is also called commerce or transaction. A mechanism that allows Trade is called a market. |
| Sampling | Sampling is that part of statistical practice concerned with the selection of individual observations intended to yield some knowledge about a population of concern, especially for the purposes of statistical inference.

Each observation measures one or more properties (weight, location, etc). of an observable entity enumerated to distinguish objects or individuals. |
| Standard deviation | In probability theory and statistics, the Standard deviation of a statistical population, a data set or a probability distribution is the square root of its being algebraically more tractable though practically less robust than the expected deviation or average absolute deviation. A low Standard deviation indicates that the data points tend to be very close to the mean, whereas high Standard deviation indicates that the data are spread out over a large range of values. |
| Depreciation | Composite life equals the total Depreciable Cost divided by the total Depreciation Per Year. \$5,900 / \$1,300 = 4.5 years.

Composite Depreciation Rate equals Depreciation Per Year divided by total Historical Cost. |
| Returns to scale | In economics, Returns to scale and economies of scale are related terms that describe what happens as the scale of production increases. They are different terms and should not be used interchangeably. . |

Production	Production refers to the economic process of converting of inputs into outputs and is a field of study in microeconomics. Production uses resources to create a good or service that is suitable for exchange. This can include manufacturing, storing, shipping, and packaging.
Anecdotal value	In economics, Anecdotal value refers to the primarily social and political value of an anecdote or anecdotal evidence in promoting understanding of a social, cultural, in the last several decades the evaluation of anecdotes has received sustained academic scrutiny from economists and scholars such as S.G. Checkland (on David Ricardo), Steven Novella, Hollis Robbins, R. Charleton, Kwamena Kwansah-Aidoo, and others; these academics seek to quantify the value inherent in the deployment of anecdotes. More recently, economists studying choice models have begun assessing Anecdotal value in the context of framing; Kahneman and Tversky suggest that choice models may be contingent on stories or anecdotes that frame or influence choice.
Per capita Income	per capita income means how much each individual receives, in monetary terms, of the yearly income generated in the country. This is what each citizen is to receive if the yearly national income is divided equally among everyone. per capita income is usually reported in units of currency per year.
Diminishing returns	In economics, Diminishing returns refers to how the marginal production of a factor of production, in contrast to the increase that would otherwise be normally expected, actually starts to progressively decrease the more of the factor are added. According to this relationship, in a production system with fixed and variable inputs (say factory size and labor), beyond some point, each additional unit of the variable input (IE man*hours) yields smaller and smaller increases in outputs, also reducing the mean productivity of each worker. Conversely, producing one more unit of output, costs more and more (due to the major amount of variable inputs being used, to little effect) This concept is also known as the law of diminishing marginal returns or the law of increasing relative cost.
Distribution	Distribution in economics refers to the way total output or income is distributed among individuals or among the factors of production (labor, land, and capital) (Samuelson and Nordhaus, 2001, p. 762). In general theory and the national income and product accounts, each unit of output corresponds to a unit of income. One use of national accounts is for classifying factor incomes and measuring their respective shares, as in National Income.
Rate of return	Yield is the compound Rate of return that includes the effect of reinvesting interest or dividends. To the right is an example of a stock investment of one share purchased at the beginning of the year for $100. · The quarterly dividend is reinvested at the quarter-end stock price. · The number of shares purchased each quarter = ($ Dividend)/($ Stock Price). · The final investment value of $103.02 is a 3.02% Yield on the initial investment of $100. This is the compound yield, and this return can be considered to be the return on the investment of $100. To calculate the Rate of return, the investor includes the reinvested dividends in the total investment. The investor received a total of $4.06 in dividends over the year, all of which were reinvested, so the investment amount increased by $4.06. · Total Investment = Cost Basis = $100 + $4.06 = $104.06. · Capital gain/loss = $103.02 - $104.06 = -$1.04 (a capital loss) · ($4.06 dividends - $1.04 capital loss) / $104.06 total investment = 2.9% ROI The disadvantage of this ROI calculation is that it does not take into account the fact that not all the money was invested during the entire year (the dividend reinvestments occurred throughout the year).

Literacy	Literacy is a concept claimed and defined by a range of different theoretical fields. In everyday terms, "Literacy" is typically described as the ability to read and write. The United Nations Educational, Scientific and Cultural Organization (UNESCO) has drafted a definition of Literacy as the "ability to identify, understand, interpret, create, communicate, compute and use printed and written materials associated with varying contexts.
Capital accumulation	Most generally, the accumulation of capital refers simply to the gathering or amassment of objects of value; the increase in wealth; or the creation of wealth. Capital can be generally defined as assets invested with the expectation that their value will increase, usually because there is the expectation of profit, rent, interest, royalties, capital gain or some other kind of return.
	The definition of Capital accumulation is subject to controversy and ambiguities, because it could refer to a net addition to existing wealth, or to a redistribution of wealth.
Returns to scale	In economics, Returns to scale and economies of scale are related terms that describe what happens as the scale of production increases. They are different terms and should not be used interchangeably. .
Endogenous Growth	In economics, Endogenous growth theory or new growth theory was developed in the 1980s as a response to criticism of the neo-classical growth model.
	In neo-classical growth models, the long-run rate of growth is exogenously determined by either assuming a savings rate (the Harrod-Domar model) or a rate of technical progress (Solow model). However, the savings rate and rate of technological progress remain unexplained.
Factor	A factor or limiting resource is a factor that controls a process, such as organism growth or species population, size, or distribution. The availability of food, predation pressure, or availability of shelter are examples of factors that could be limiting for an organism. An example of a limiting factor is sunlight, which is crucial in rainforests.
Factors of Production	In economics, Factors of production (or productive inputs) are the resources employed to produce goods and services. They facilitate production but do not become part of the product (as with raw materials) or are significantly transformed by the production process (as with fuel used to power machinery). To 19th century economists, the Factors of production were land , labor (the ability to work), and capital goods (human-made tools and equipment).
Patent	Patents are legal instruments intended to encourage innovation by providing a limited "monopoly" to the inventor (or their assignee) in return for the disclosure of the invention. The underlying assumption being innovation is encouraged because an inventor can secure exclusive rights, and therefore a higher probability of financial rewards in the market place. The publication of the invention is mandatory to get a Patent.
Research and development	The phrase Research and development, according to the Organization for Economic Co-operation and Development, refers to "creative work undertaken on a systematic basis in order to increase the stock of knowledge, including knowledge of man, culture and society, and the use of this stock of knowledge to devise new applications"
	New product design and development is more often than not a crucial factor in the survival of a company. In an industry that is fast changing, firms must continually revise their design and range of products. This is necessary due to continuous technology change and development as well as other competitors and the changing preference of customers.

Production function	In economics, a Production function is a function that specifies the output of a firm, an industry) compares the practice of the existing entities converting inputs X into output y to determine the most efficient practice Production function of the existing entities, whether the most efficient feasible practice production or the most efficient actual practice production. In either case, the maximum output of a technologically-determined production process is a mathematical function of input factors of production.
Productivity	Productivity is a measure of output from a production process, per unit of input. For example, lab is typically measured as a ratio of output per labor-hour, an input. Productivity may be conceived of as a metric of the technical or engineering efficiency of production.
Competition	Co-operative Competition is based upon promoting mutual survival - "everyone wins". Adam Smith"s "invisible hand" is a process where individuals compete to improve their level of happiness but compete in a cooperative manner through peaceful exchange and without violating other people. Cooperative Competition focuses individuals/groups/organisms against the environment.
Externality	In economics, an Externality or spillover of an economic transaction is an impact on a party that is not directly involved in the transaction. In such a case, prices do not reflect the full costs or benefits in production or consumption of a product or service. An advantageous impact is called an external benefit or positive Externality, while a detrimental impact is called an external cost or negative Externality.
Belief	Belief is the psychological state in which an individual holds a proposition or premise to be true. The terms Belief and knowledge are used differently in philosophy. Epistemology is the philosophical study of knowledge and Belief.
Total-factor productivity	In economics, total-factor productivity (TFP) is a variable which accounts for effects in total output not caused by inputs. For example, a year with unusually good weather will tend to have higher output, because bad weather hinders agricultural output. A variable like weather does not directly relate to unit inputs, so weather is considered a total-factor productivity variable.
Marginal product	In economics, the Marginal product or marginal physical product is the extra output produced by one more unit of an input . Assuming that no other inputs to production change, the Marginal product of a given input (X) can be expressed as: Marginal product = $\Delta Y/\Delta X$ = (the change of Y)/(the change of X). In neoclassical economics, this is the mathematical derivative of the production function....
Marginal product of Labor	In economics, the Marginal product of labor also known as MPL or MPN is the change in output from hiring one additional unit of labor. It is the increase in output added by the last unit of labor. Assuming that no other inputs to production change, the marginal product of a given input (X) can be expressed as: MP = $\Delta Y/\Delta X$ = (the change of Y)/(the change of X). · There is a factory which produces toys.

Share	In financial markets, a Share is a unit of account for various financial instruments including stocks (ordinary or preferential), and investments in limited partnerships, and REITs. The common feature of all these is equity participation (limited in the case of preference Shares). In American English, the plural stocks is widely used instead of Shares, in other words to refer to the stock (or perhaps originally stock certificates) of even a single company.
Labor force	In economics, the people in the Labor force are the suppliers of labor. The Labor force is all the nonmilitary people who are employed or unemployed. In 2005, the worldwide Labor force was over 3 billion people.
Trade	Trade is the voluntary exchange of goods, services, or both. Trade is also called commerce or transaction. A mechanism that allows Trade is called a market.

Distribution	Distribution in economics refers to the way total output or income is distributed among individuals or among the factors of production (labor, land, and capital) (Samuelson and Nordhaus, 2001, p. 762). In general theory and the national income and product accounts, each unit of output corresponds to a unit of income. One use of national accounts is for classifying factor incomes and measuring their respective shares, as in National Income.
Externality	In economics, an Externality or spillover of an economic transaction is an impact on a party that is not directly involved in the transaction. In such a case, prices do not reflect the full costs or benefits in production or consumption of a product or service. An advantageous impact is called an external benefit or positive Externality, while a detrimental impact is called an external cost or negative Externality.
Cost	In business, retail, and accounting, a cost is the value of money that has been used up to produce something, and hence is not available for use anymore. In economics, a cost is an alternative that is given up as a result of a decision. In business, the cost may be one of acquisition, in which case the amount of money expended to acquire it is counted as cost.
Capital accumulation	Most generally, the accumulation of capital refers simply to the gathering or amassment of objects of value; the increase in wealth; or the creation of wealth. Capital can be generally defined as assets invested with the expectation that their value will increase, usually because there is the expectation of profit, rent, interest, royalties, capital gain or some other kind of return. The definition of Capital accumulation is subject to controversy and ambiguities, because it could refer to a net addition to existing wealth, or to a redistribution of wealth.
Loan	A Loan is a type of debt. Like all debt instruments, a Loan entails the redistribution of financial assets over time, between the lender and the borrower. In a Loan, the borrower initially receives or borrows an amount of money, called the principal, from the lender, and is obligated to pay back or repay an equal amount of money to the lender at a later time.
Rate of return	Yield is the compound Rate of return that includes the effect of reinvesting interest or dividends. To the right is an example of a stock investment of one share purchased at the beginning of the year for $100. · The quarterly dividend is reinvested at the quarter-end stock price. · The number of shares purchased each quarter = ($ Dividend)/($ Stock Price). · The final investment value of $103.02 is a 3.02% Yield on the initial investment of $100. This is the compound yield, and this return can be considered to be the return on the investment of $100. To calculate the Rate of return, the investor includes the reinvested dividends in the total investment. The investor received a total of $4.06 in dividends over the year, all of which were reinvested, so the investment amount increased by $4.06. · Total Investment = Cost Basis = $100 + $4.06 = $104.06. · Capital gain/loss = $103.02 - $104.06 = -$1.04 (a capital loss) · ($4.06 dividends - $1.04 capital loss) / $104.06 total investment = 2.9% ROI The disadvantage of this ROI calculation is that it does not take into account the fact that not all the money was invested during the entire year (the dividend reinvestments occurred throughout the year).

Coordination failure	Coordination failure is the electoral problem resulting from competition between two or more candidates or political parties from the same or approximate location in the political ideological spectrum or space against an opposing candidate or political party from the other side of the political ideological spectrum or space. The resulting fragmentation of political support may result in electoral defeat. Coordination failures, and thus political calculations attempting to avoid them, appear most frequently in elections involving executives and representatives from single member districts.
Coordination game	In game theory, Coordination games are a class of games with multiple pure strategy Nash equilibria in which players choose the same or corresponding strategies. Coordination games are a formalization of the idea of a coordination problem, which is widespread in the social sciences, including economics, meaning situations in which all parties can realize mutual gains, but only by making mutually consistent decisions. A common application is the choice of technological standards.
Demand	In economics, demand is the desire to own anything and the ability to pay for it. . The term demand signifies the ability or the willingness to buy a particular commodity at a given point of time.
Marshall Plan	The Marshall Plan was the primary plan of the United States for rebuilding and creating a stronger foundation for the countries of Western Europe, and repelling communism after World War II. The initiative was named for Secretary of State George Marshall and was largely the creation of State Department officials, especially William L. Clayton and George F. Kennan. George Marshall spoke of the administration"s desire to help European recovery in his address at Harvard University in June 1947.
	The reconstruction plan, developed at a meeting of the participating European states, was established on June 5, 1947. It offered the same aid to the USSR and its allies, but they did not accept it. The plan was in operation for four years beginning in April 1948. During that period some USD 13 billion in economic and technical assistance were given to help the recovery of the European countries that had joined in the Organization for European Economic Co-operation.
Saleability	Saleability is a technical analysis term used to compare performances of different trading systems or different investments within one system. Note, it is not simply another word for profit. There are varying definitions for it, some as simple as the expected or average ratio of revenue to cost for a particular investment or trading system or "ratio of the number of winning trades or investments to the total number of trades or investments made, a number ranging from zero to 1." Others can be complex or counter-intuitive.
Industry	An industry is the manufacturing of a good or service within a category. Although industry is a broad term for any kind of economic production, in economics and urban planning industry is a synonym for the secondary sector, which is a type of economic activity involved in the manufacturing of raw materials into goods and products.
	There are four key industrial economic sectors: the primary sector, largely raw material extraction industries such as mining and farming; the secondary sector, involving refining, construction, and manufacturing; the tertiary sector, which deals with services and distribution of manufactured goods; and the quaternary sector, a relatively new type of knowledge industry focusing on technological research, design and development such as computer programming, and biochemistry.
Mahalanobis model	The Mahalanobis model is a model of economic development, created by Indian statistician Prasanta Chandra Mahalanobis in 1953. Mahalanobis became essentially the key economist of India"s Second Five Year Plan, becoming subject to much of India"s most dramatic economic debates.

	The essence of the model is a shift in the pattern of industrial investment towards building up a domestic consumption goods sector. Thus the strategy suggests in order to reach a high standard in consumption, investment in building a capacity in the production of capital goods is firstly needed.
Year	A year is the amount of time it takes the Earth to make one revolution around the Sun. By extension, this can be applied to any planet: for example, a "Martian year" is the time in which Mars completes its own orbit.
	Although there is no universally accepted symbol for the year, NIST SP811 and ISO 80000-3:2006 suggest the symbol a in the International System of Units.
Returns to scale	In economics, Returns to scale and economies of scale are related terms that describe what happens as the scale of production increases. They are different terms and should not be used interchangeably. .
Capital market	A Capital market is a market for securities (both debt and equity), where business enterprises (companies) and governments can raise long-term funds. It is defined as a market in which money is lent for periods longer than a year, as the raising of short-term funds takes place on other markets (e.g., the money market). The Capital market includes the stock market (equity securities) and the bond market (debt).
Anecdotal value	In economics, Anecdotal value refers to the primarily social and political value of an anecdote or anecdotal evidence in promoting understanding of a social, cultural, in the last several decades the evaluation of anecdotes has received sustained academic scrutiny from economists and scholars such as S.G. Checkland (on David Ricardo), Steven Novella, Hollis Robbins, R. Charleton, Kwamena Kwansah-Aidoo, and others; these academics seek to quantify the value inherent in the deployment of anecdotes. More recently, economists studying choice models have begun assessing Anecdotal value in the context of framing; Kahneman and Tversky suggest that choice models may be contingent on stories or anecdotes that frame or influence choice.
Competition	Co-operative Competition is based upon promoting mutual survival - "everyone wins". Adam Smith"s "invisible hand" is a process where individuals compete to improve their level of happiness but compete in a cooperative manner through peaceful exchange and without violating other people. Cooperative Competition focuses individuals/groups/organisms against the environment.
Productivity	Productivity is a measure of output from a production process, per unit of input. For example, lab is typically measured as a ratio of output per labor-hour, an input. Productivity may be conceived of as a metric of the technical or engineering efficiency of production.
Trade	Trade is the voluntary exchange of goods, services, or both. Trade is also called commerce or transaction. A mechanism that allows Trade is called a market.
International Trade	International trade is exchange of capital, goods, and services across international borders or territories. In most countries, it represents a significant share of gross domestic product (GDP). While International trade has been present throughout much of history , its economic, social, and political importance has been on the rise in recent centuries.
Multilateralism	multilateralism is a term in international relations that refers to multiple countries working in concert on a given issue.

	Most international organizations, such as the United Nations (UN) and the World Trade Organization are multilateral in nature. The main proponents of multilateralism have traditionally been the middle powers such as Canada, Australia, Switzerland, the Benelux countries and the Nordic countries.
Dot-com bubble	The "Dot-com bubble" (or) was a speculative bubble covering roughly 1998-2001 (with a climax on March 10, 2000 with the NASDAQ peaking at 5132.52) during which stock markets in Western nations saw their equity value rise rapidly from growth in the more recent Internet sector and related fields. While the latter part was a boom and bust cycle, the Internet boom sometimes is meant to refer to the steady commercial growth of the Internet with the advent of the world wide web as exemplified by the first release of the Mosaic web browser in 1993 and continuing through the 1990s.
	The period was marked by the founding (and, in many cases, spectacular failure) of a group of new Internet-based companies commonly referred to as dot-coms.
Correlation	In statistics, Correlation (often measured as a Correlation coefficient, ρ) indicates the strength and direction of a linear relationship between two random variables. That is in contrast with the usage of the term in colloquial speech, which denotes any relationship, not necessarily linear. In general statistical usage, Correlation or co-relation refers to the departure of two random variables from independence.
Cost-benefit	cost-benefit analysis is a term that refers both to:
	· helping to appraise, or assess, the case for a project or proposal, which itself is a process known as project appraisal; and · an informal approach to making decisions of any kind. Under both definitions the process involves, whether explicitly or implicitly, weighing the total expected costs against the total expected benefits of one or more actions in order to choose the best or most profitable option. The formal process is often referred to as either CBA (cost-benefit Analysis) or BCA (Benefit-Cost Analysis).
Cost-benefit analysis	Cost-benefit analysis is a term that refers both to:
	· helping to appraise, or assess, the case for a project or proposal, which itself is a process known as project appraisal; and · an informal approach to making decisions of any kind. Under both definitions the process involves, whether explicitly or implicitly, weighing the total expected costs against the total expected benefits of one or more actions in order to choose the best or most profitable option. The formal process is often referred to as either CBA (Cost-benefit analysis) or BCA (Benefit-Cost Analysis).

Income distribution	In economics, the Lorenz curve is a graphical representation of the cumulative distribution function of a probability distribution; it is a graph showing the proportion of the distribution assumed by the bottom y% of the values. It is often used to represent income Distribution, where it shows for the bottom x% of households, what percentage y% of the total income they have. The percentage of households is plotted on the x-axis, the percentage of income on the y-axis.
Distribution of Wealth	Distribution of wealth is a comparison of the wealth of various members or groups in a society. It differs from the distribution of income in a manner analogous to the difference between position and speed. Wealth is a person"s net worth, expressed as: wealth = assets - liabilities The word "wealth" is often confused with "income".
Inequality	In mathematics, an inequality is a statement about the relative size or order of two objects
Anecdotal value	In economics, Anecdotal value refers to the primarily social and political value of an anecdote or anecdotal evidence in promoting understanding of a social, cultural, in the last several decades the evaluation of anecdotes has received sustained academic scrutiny from economists and scholars such as S.G. Checkland (on David Ricardo), Steven Novella, Hollis Robbins, R. Charleton, Kwamena Kwansah-Aidoo, and others; these academics seek to quantify the value inherent in the deployment of anecdotes. More recently, economists studying choice models have begun assessing Anecdotal value in the context of framing; Kahneman and Tversky suggest that choice models may be contingent on stories or anecdotes that frame or influence choice.
Economic Inequality	Economic inequality comprises all disparities in the distribution of economic assets and income. The term typically refers to inequality among individuals and groups within a society, but can also refer to inequality among countries. Economic inequality generally refers to equality of outcome, and is related to the idea of equality of opportunity.
Asset	In business and accounting, Assets are economic resources owned by business or company. Anything tangible or intangible that one possesses, usually considered as applicable to the payment of one"s debts is considered an Asset. Simplistically stated, Assets are things of value that can be readily converted into cash (although cash itself is also considered an Asset).
Production	Production refers to the economic process of converting of inputs into outputs and is a field of study in microeconomics. Production uses resources to create a good or service that is suitable for exchange. This can include manufacturing, storing, shipping, and packaging.
Factor	A factor or limiting resource is a factor that controls a process, such as organism growth or species population, size, or distribution. The availability of food, predation pressure, or availability of shelter are examples of factors that could be limiting for an organism. An example of a limiting factor is sunlight, which is crucial in rainforests.
Factors of Production	In economics, Factors of production (or productive inputs) are the resources employed to produce goods and services. They facilitate production but do not become part of the product (as with raw materials) or are significantly transformed by the production process (as with fuel used to power machinery). To 19th century economists, the Factors of production were land , labor (the ability to work), and capital goods (human-made tools and equipment).

Distribution	Distribution in economics refers to the way total output or income is distributed among individuals or among the factors of production (labor, land, and capital) (Samuelson and Nordhaus, 2001, p. 762). In general theory and the national income and product accounts, each unit of output corresponds to a unit of income. One use of national accounts is for classifying factor incomes and measuring their respective shares, as in National Income.
Distribution of Income	The concept of inequality is distinct from that of poverty and fairness. Income inequality metrics or income distribution metrics are used by social scientists to measure the Distribution of income, and economic inequality among the participants in a particular economy, such as that of a specific country or of the world in general. While different theories may try to explain how income inequality comes about, income inequality metrics simply provide a system of measurement used to determine the dispersion of incomes.
Share	In financial markets, a Share is a unit of account for various financial instruments including stocks (ordinary or preferential), and investments in limited partnerships, and REITs. The common feature of all these is equity participation (limited in the case of preference Shares).
	In American English, the plural stocks is widely used instead of Shares, in other words to refer to the stock (or perhaps originally stock certificates) of even a single company.
Mean	In statistics, mean has two related meanings:
	· the arithmetic mean .
	· the expected value of a random variable, which is also called the population mean.
	It is sometimes stated that the "mean" means average. This is incorrect if "mean" is taken in the specific sense of "arithmetic mean" as there are different types of averages: the mean, median, and mode.
Absolute deviation	In statistics, the absolute deviation of an element of a data set is the absolute difference between that element and a given point. Typically the point from which the deviation is measured is a measure of central tendency, most often the median or sometimes the mean of the data set.
	$D_i = \mid x_i - m(X) \mid$
	where
	D_i is the absolute deviation,
	x_i is the data element
	and m(X) is the chosen measure of central tendency of the data set--sometimes the mean ($\overline{x}$), but most often the median.
Coefficient of variation	In probability theory and statistics, the Coefficient of variation (CV) is a normalized measure of dispersion of a probability distribution. It is defined as the ratio of the standard deviation σ to the mean μ:
	$$c_v = \frac{\sigma}{\mu}$$
	This is only defined for non-zero mean, and is most useful for variables that are always positive. It is also known as unitized risk.

Measure | The measures used in economics are physical measures, nominal price value measures and fixed price value measures. These measures differ from one another by the variables they measure and by the variables excluded from measurements. The measurable variables in economics are quantity, quality and distribution.

Inequality	In mathematics, an inequality is a statement about the relative size or order of two objects
Supply and demand	Supply and demand is an economic model based on price, utility and quantity in a market. It concludes that in a competitive market, price will function to equalize the quantity demanded by consumers, and the quantity supplied by producers, resulting in an economic equilibrium of price and quantity. The demand schedule, depicted graphically as the demand curve, represents the amount of goods that buyers are willing and able to purchase at various prices, assuming all other non-price factors remain the same.
Distribution	Distribution in economics refers to the way total output or income is distributed among individuals or among the factors of production (labor, land, and capital) (Samuelson and Nordhaus, 2001, p. 762). In general theory and the national income and product accounts, each unit of output corresponds to a unit of income. One use of national accounts is for classifying factor incomes and measuring their respective shares, as in National Income.
Distribution of Wealth	Distribution of wealth is a comparison of the wealth of various members or groups in a society. It differs from the distribution of income in a manner analogous to the difference between position and speed. Wealth is a person"s net worth, expressed as: wealth = assets - liabilities The word "wealth" is often confused with "income".
Per capita Income	per capita income means how much each individual receives, in monetary terms, of the yearly income generated in the country. This is what each citizen is to receive if the yearly national income is divided equally among everyone. per capita income is usually reported in units of currency per year.
Share	In financial markets, a Share is a unit of account for various financial instruments including stocks (ordinary or preferential), and investments in limited partnerships, and REITs. The common feature of all these is equity participation (limited in the case of preference Shares). In American English, the plural stocks is widely used instead of Shares, in other words to refer to the stock (or perhaps originally stock certificates) of even a single company.
Dot-com bubble	The "Dot-com bubble" (or) was a speculative bubble covering roughly 1998-2001 (with a climax on March 10, 2000 with the NASDAQ peaking at 5132.52) during which stock markets in Western nations saw their equity value rise rapidly from growth in the more recent Internet sector and related fields. While the latter part was a boom and bust cycle, the Internet boom sometimes is meant to refer to the steady commercial growth of the Internet with the advent of the world wide web as exemplified by the first release of the Mosaic web browser in 1993 and continuing through the 1990s. The period was marked by the founding (and, in many cases, spectacular failure) of a group of new Internet-based companies commonly referred to as dot-coms.
Tunnel Effect	In experimental psychology, the Tunnel effect is the perception as a single object of something moving beyond an occluding object and then reappearing after a suitable amount of time on the other side of it. This phenomenon has been studied by Burke (1952), who discovered that the optimal amount of time for giving the impression of a single object is shorter what is actually needed to cross the occlusion at that speed.
Gross national product	A variety of measures of national income and output are used in economics to estimate total economic activity in a country or region, including gross domestic product (GDP), Gross National Product , and net national income (NNI).

	There are three main ways of calculating these numbers; the output approach, the income approach and the expenditure approach. In theory, the three must yield the same, because total expenditures on goods and services must equal the total income paid to the producers (GNI), and that must also equal the total value of the output of goods and services .
Trade	Trade is the voluntary exchange of goods, services, or both. Trade is also called commerce or transaction. A mechanism that allows Trade is called a market.
Income distribution	In economics, the Lorenz curve is a graphical representation of the cumulative distribution function of a probability distribution; it is a graph showing the proportion of the distribution assumed by the bottom y% of the values. It is often used to represent income Distribution, where it shows for the bottom x% of households, what percentage y% of the total income they have. The percentage of households is plotted on the x-axis, the percentage of income on the y-axis.
Coefficient of variation	In probability theory and statistics, the Coefficient of variation (CV) is a normalized measure of dispersion of a probability distribution. It is defined as the ratio of the standard deviation σ to the mean μ: $$c_v = \frac{\sigma}{\mu}$$ This is only defined for non-zero mean, and is most useful for variables that are always positive. It is also known as unitized risk.
Time series	In statistics, signal processing, and many other fields, a Time series is a sequence of data points, measured typically at successive times, spaced at (often uniform) time intervals. Time series analysis comprises methods that attempt to understand such Time series, often either to understand the underlying context of the data points (Where did they come from? What generated them?), or to make forecasts (predictions). Time series forecasting is the use of a model to forecast future events based on known past events: to forecast future data points before they are measured.
Dual economy	A Dual economy is the existence of two separate economic systems within one country. Dual economies are common in less developed countries, where one system is geared to local needs and another to the global export market. Dual economies need not be across economic sector boundaries.
Wage	Several countries have enacted a statutory minimum Wage rate that sets a price floor for certain kinds of labor. Wage derives from words which suggest "making a promise," often in monetary form. Specifically from the Old French word wagier or gagier meaning to pledge or promise, from which the money placed in a bet also derives.
Redistribution	In economics, redistribution is the transfer of income, wealth or property from some individuals to others. Income redistribution evens the amount of income that individuals are permitted to earn, in order to correct the ineffectiveness of a market economy to remunerate based on the amount of labor expended by an individual. The objective of moderate income redistribution is to avoid the unjust equalization of incomes on one side and unjust extremes of concentration on the other sides.
Wage rate	Several countries have enacted a statutory minimum wage rate that sets a price floor for certain kinds of labor.

Wage derives from words which suggest "making a promise," often in monetary form. Specifically from the Old French word wagier or gagier meaning to pledge or promise, from which the money placed in a bet also derives.

Anecdotal value

In economics, Anecdotal value refers to the primarily social and political value of an anecdote or anecdotal evidence in promoting understanding of a social, cultural, in the last several decades the evaluation of anecdotes has received sustained academic scrutiny from economists and scholars such as S.G. Checkland (on David Ricardo), Steven Novella, Hollis Robbins, R. Charleton, Kwamena Kwansah-Aidoo, and others; these academics seek to quantify the value inherent in the deployment of anecdotes. More recently, economists studying choice models have begun assessing Anecdotal value in the context of framing; Kahneman and Tversky suggest that choice models may be contingent on stories or anecdotes that frame or influence choice.

Economic Growth

Economic growth is an increase in activity in an economy. It is often measured as the rate of change of gross domestic product (GDP). Economic growth refers only to the quantity of goods and services produced; it says nothing about the way in which they are produced.

Needs

The most widely known academic model of Needs was proposed by psychologist Abraham Maslow. In his theory, he proposed that people have a hierarchy of psychological Needs, which range from security to self-actualization. However, while this model is intuitively appealing, it has been difficult to operationalize it experimentally.

Conspicuous Consumption

Conspicuous consumption is a term used to describe the lavish spending on goods and services acquired mainly for the purpose of displaying income or wealth. In the mind of a conspicuous consumer, such display serves as a means of attaining or maintaining social status. A very similar but more colloquial term is "keeping up with the Joneses".

Standard of living

Standard of living is generally measured by standards such as real (i.e. inflation adjusted) income per person and poverty rate. Other measures such as access and quality of health care, income growth inequality and educational standards are also used. Examples are access to certain goods (such as number of refrigerators per 1000 people), or measures of health such as life expectancy.

Economic Inequality

Economic inequality comprises all disparities in the distribution of economic assets and income. The term typically refers to inequality among individuals and groups within a society, but can also refer to inequality among countries. Economic inequality generally refers to equality of outcome, and is related to the idea of equality of opportunity.

Land reform

Land reforms (also agrarian reform, though that can have a broader meaning) is an often-controversial alteration in the societal arrangements whereby government administers possession and use of land. Land reform may consist of a government-initiated or government-backed real estate property redistribution, generally of agricultural land, or be part of an even more revolutionary program that may include forcible removal of an existing government that is seen to oppose such reforms.

Throughout history, popular discontent with land-related institutions has been one of the most common factors in provoking revolutionary movements and other social upheavals.

Tax sale

A Tax sale refers to property (usually real property) being sold by a taxing authority or the court to recover delinquent taxes. In the Tax sale arena, the taxing jurisdiction is usually the county (the parish in the case of Louisiana, or cities, towns, townships (commonly in the New England states area) - even school districts initiate Tax sales in Texas).

	Two main methods are used by counties to capture delinquent real property tax: tax deed auctions/sales, or tax lien certificate sales/auctions.
Increment	An increment is an increase of some amount, either fixed or variable. For example one"s salary may have a fixed annual increment or one based on a percentage of its current value. A decrease is called a decrement.
Rate of return	Yield is the compound Rate of return that includes the effect of reinvesting interest or dividends.
	To the right is an example of a stock investment of one share purchased at the beginning of the year for $100.
	· The quarterly dividend is reinvested at the quarter-end stock price. · The number of shares purchased each quarter = ($ Dividend)/($ Stock Price). · The final investment value of $103.02 is a 3.02% Yield on the initial investment of $100. This is the compound yield, and this return can be considered to be the return on the investment of $100.
	To calculate the Rate of return, the investor includes the reinvested dividends in the total investment. The investor received a total of $4.06 in dividends over the year, all of which were reinvested, so the investment amount increased by $4.06.
	· Total Investment = Cost Basis = $100 + $4.06 = $104.06. · Capital gain/loss = $103.02 - $104.06 = -$1.04 (a capital loss) · ($4.06 dividends - $1.04 capital loss) / $104.06 total investment = 2.9% ROI
	The disadvantage of this ROI calculation is that it does not take into account the fact that not all the money was invested during the entire year (the dividend reinvestments occurred throughout the year).
Lump-sum Tax	A Lump-sum tax is a tax that is a fixed amount no matter what the change in circumstance of the taxed entity. (A lump-sum subsidy or lump-sum redistribution is defined similarly). It is a regressive tax, such that the lower income is, the higher percentage of income applicable to the tax.
Asset	In business and accounting, Assets are economic resources owned by business or company. Anything tangible or intangible that one possesses, usually considered as applicable to the payment of one"s debts is considered an Asset. Simplistically stated, Assets are things of value that can be readily converted into cash (although cash itself is also considered an Asset).
Final good	In economics final goods are goods that are ultimately consumed rather than used in the production of another good. For example, a car sold to a consumer is a final good; the components such as tires sold to the car manufacturer are not; they are intermediate goods used to make the final good.
	When used in measures of national income and output the term final goods only includes new goods.
Demand	In economics, demand is the desire to own anything and the ability to pay for it. . The term demand signifies the ability or the willingness to buy a particular commodity at a given point of time.
Luxury good	In economics, a luxury good is a good for which demand increases more than proportionally as income rises, in contrast to a "necessity good", for which demand increases less than proportionally as income rises.

luxury goods are said to have high income elasticity of demand: as people become wealthier, they will buy more and more of the luxury good. This also means, however, that should there be a decline in income its demand will drop.

Derived Demand	Derived demand is a term in economics, where demand for one good or service occurs as a result of demand for another. This may occur as the former is a part of production of the second. For example, demand for coal leads to Derived demand for mining, as coal must be mined for coal to be consumed.
Factor	A factor or limiting resource is a factor that controls a process, such as organism growth or species population, size, or distribution. The availability of food, predation pressure, or availability of shelter are examples of factors that could be limiting for an organism. An example of a limiting factor is sunlight, which is crucial in rainforests.
Capital market	A Capital market is a market for securities (both debt and equity), where business enterprises (companies) and governments can raise long-term funds. It is defined as a market in which money is lent for periods longer than a year, as the raising of short-term funds takes place on other markets (e.g., the money market). The Capital market includes the stock market (equity securities) and the bond market (debt).
Bond market	The Bond market is a financial market where participants buy and sell debt securities, usually in the form of bonds. As of 2008, the size of the international Bond market is an estimated $67.0 trillion , of which the size of the outstanding U.S. Bond market debt was $33.5 trillion.
	Nearly all of the $923 billion average daily trading volume (as of early 2007) in the U.S. Bond market takes place between broker-dealers and large institutions in a decentralized, over-the-counter (OTC) market.
Credit rating	A Credit rating estimates the credit worthiness of an individual, corporation, prepared by a credit bureau at the request of the lender (Black"s Law Dictionary).
Loan	A Loan is a type of debt. Like all debt instruments, a Loan entails the redistribution of financial assets over time, between the lender and the borrower.
	In a Loan, the borrower initially receives or borrows an amount of money, called the principal, from the lender, and is obligated to pay back or repay an equal amount of money to the lender at a later time.
Social contract	social contract describes a broad class of theories that try to explain the ways in which people form states and/or maintain social order. The notion of the social contract implies that the people give up some rights to a government or other authority in order to receive or maintain social order through the rule of law. It can also be thought of as an agreement by the governed on a set of rules by which they are governed.
Cost	In business, retail, and accounting, a cost is the value of money that has been used up to produce something, and hence is not available for use anymore. In economics, a cost is an alternative that is given up as a result of a decision. In business, the cost may be one of acquisition, in which case the amount of money expended to acquire it is counted as cost.
Entrepreneurship	For Frank H. Knight (1921) and Peter Drucker (1970) Entrepreneurship is about taking risk. The behavior of the entrepreneur reflects a kind of person willing to put his or her career and financial security on the line and take risks in the name of an idea, spending much time as well as capital on an uncertain venture. Knight classified three types of uncertainty.

· Risk, which is measurable statistically .

· Ambiguity, which is hard to measure statistically .

· True Uncertainty or Knightian Uncertainty, which is impossible to estimate or predict statistically .

Choice

There are four types of decisions, although they can be expressed in different ways. Brian Tracy, who often uses enumerated lists in his talks, breaks them down into:

· Command decisions, which can only be made by you, as the "Commander in Chief"; or owner of a company.

· Delegated decisions, which may be made by anyone, such as the color of the bike shed, and should be delegated, as the decision must be made but the Choice is inconsequential.

· Avoided decisions, where the outcome could be so severe that the Choice should not be made, as the consequences can not be recovered from if the wrong Choice is made. This will most likely result in negative actions, such as death.

· "No-brainer" decisions, where the Choice is so obvious that only one Choice can reasonably be made.

A fifth type, however, or fourth if three and four are combined as one type, is the collaborative decision, which should be made in consultation with, and by agreement of others.

Price-specie-flow mechanism

The price-specie-flow mechanism is a logical argument by David Hume against the Mercantilist (1700-1776) idea that a nation should strive for a positive balance of trade, a system in which gold is the official means of international payments and each nation"s currency is in the form of gold itself or of paper currency fully convertible into gold.

Hume argued that when a country with a gold standard had a positive balance of trade, gold would flow into the country in the amount that the value of exports exceeds the value of imports.

Net Profit

In business and finance accounting, net profit is equal to the gross profit minus overheads minus interest payable plus/minus one off items for a given time period (usually: accounting period).

A common synonym for "net profit" when discussing financial statements (which include a balance sheet and an income statement) is the bottom line. This term results from the traditional appearance of an income statement which shows all allocated revenues and expenses over a specified time period with the resulting summation on the bottom line of the report.

Mean

In statistics, mean has two related meanings:

· the arithmetic mean .

· the expected value of a random variable, which is also called the population mean.

It is sometimes stated that the "mean" means average. This is incorrect if "mean" is taken in the specific sense of "arithmetic mean" as there are different types of averages: the mean, median, and mode.

Labor Supply

In mainstream economic theories, the Labor supply is the number of total hours that workers wish to work at a given real wage rate. Realistically, the Labor supply is a function of various factors within an economy. For instance, overpopulation increases the number of available workers driving down wages and can result in high unemployment.

Preference	Preference is a concept, used in the social sciences, particularly economics. It assumes a real or imagined "choice" between alternatives and the possibility of rank ordering of these alternatives, based on happiness, satisfaction, gratification, enjoyment, utility they provide. More generally, it can be seen as a source of motivation.
Demand curve	In economics, the Demand curve can be defined as the graph depicting the relationship between the price of a certain commodity, and the amount of it that consumers are willing and able to purchase at that given price. It is a graphic representation of a demand schedule. The Demand curve for all consumers together follows from the Demand curve of every individual consumer: the individual demands at each price are added together.
Market equilibrium	In economics, economic equilibrium is simply a state of the world where economic forces are balanced and in the absence of external influences the (equilibrium) values of economic variables will not change. It is the point at which quantity demanded and quantity supplied are equal. Market equilibrium, for example, refers to a condition where a market price is established through competition such that the amount of goods or services sought by buyers is equal to the amount of goods or services produced by sellers.
Change	changes can refer to: · A jazz term for chord progression · changes (band), an American folk band · The changes (band), an American rock band · changes (The Monkees album), The Monkees" ninth studio album · changes, Christopher Wiliams" second studio album · changes, an album by R. Carlos Nakai · changes (Taylor Horn album), Taylor Horn"s third studio album · changesbowie, a David Bowie compilation album · changes (Kelly Osbourne album), Kelly Osbourne"s second studio album · changes (Vanilla Sky album), Vanilla Sky"s third album · changes (Jarrett album), by Keith Jarrett, Jack DeJohnette and Gary Peacock · changes (Billy "Crash" Craddock album) · changes (Lisa Miskovsky album) · changes (Tanya Tucker album) · changes, an album by Johnny Rivers

· "changes" (David Bowie song), a song by David Bowie on his 1971 album Hunky Dory

· "changes" (2Pac song), a song by Tupac Shakur on his Greatest Hits album

· "changes" (Black Sabbath song), a ballad by Black Sabbath, remade as a duet by Kelly and Ozzy Osbourne

· "changes" (Will Young song), a song by Will Young on his fourth studio album, Let It Go

· "changes" (Gareth Gates song), a song by Gareth Gates, from the album Pictures of the Other Side

· "changes" (Imagination song), a song by Imagination, from the album In the Heat of the Night

· "changes", a song by Yes on the album 90125

· "changes", a song by "Buddy" Miles ' Jimi Hendrix on the album Band of Gypsys

· "changes", a song by Jane"s Addiction

· "changes", a song by Phil Ochs

· "changes", a song by Godsmack on the album Faceless

· "changes", a song by The Zombies on the album Odessey and Oracle

· "changes", a song by 3 Doors Down on the album Away from the Sun

· "changes", a song by Sugar on the album Copper Blue

· "changes", a song by Chris Lake

· "changes", a song by Moby Grape on their album Moby Grape

· "changes", a song by Santana on their album Zebop!

· The changes (TV series), produced by the BBC in 1975. Also the changes Trilogy of novels on which the series was based, written by Peter Dickinson .

Nutrition

Nutrition is the provision, to cells and organisms, of the materials necessary (in the form of food) to support life. Many common health problems can be prevented or alleviated with a healthy diet.

Nutriton is a process of intake of nutrients (like carbohydrates, fats,proteins,Vitamins, minerals and water) by the organism as well as the utilisation of these nutrients by the organism.

Steady state

A system in a Steady state has numerous properties that are unchanging in time. The concept of Steady state has relevance in many fields, in particular thermodynamics. Steady state is a more general situation than dynamic equilibrium.

Anecdotal value	In economics, Anecdotal value refers to the primarily social and political value of an anecdote or anecdotal evidence in promoting understanding of a social, cultural, in the last several decades the evaluation of anecdotes has received sustained academic scrutiny from economists and scholars such as S.G. Checkland (on David Ricardo), Steven Novella, Hollis Robbins, R. Charleton, Kwamena Kwansah-Aidoo, and others; these academics seek to quantify the value inherent in the deployment of anecdotes. More recently, economists studying choice models have begun assessing Anecdotal value in the context of framing; Kahneman and Tversky suggest that choice models may be contingent on stories or anecdotes that frame or influence choice.
Income distribution	In economics, the Lorenz curve is a graphical representation of the cumulative distribution function of a probability distribution; it is a graph showing the proportion of the distribution assumed by the bottom y% of the values. It is often used to represent income Distribution, where it shows for the bottom x% of households, what percentage y% of the total income they have. The percentage of households is plotted on the x-axis, the percentage of income on the y-axis.
Nutrition	Nutrition is the provision, to cells and organisms, of the materials necessary (in the form of food) to support life. Many common health problems can be prevented or alleviated with a healthy diet.
	Nutriton is a process of intake of nutrients (like carbohydrates, fats,proteins,Vitamins, minerals and water) by the organism as well as the utilisation of these nutrients by the organism.
Poverty threshold	The Poverty threshold, is the minimum level of income deemed necessary to achieve an adequate standard of living in a given country. In practice, like the definition of poverty, the official or common understanding of the poverty line is significantly higher in developed countries than in developing countries.
	The common international poverty line has been roughly $1 a day, or more precisely $1.08 at 1993 purchasing-power parity (PPP).
Mean	In statistics, mean has two related meanings:
	· the arithmetic mean .
	· the expected value of a random variable, which is also called the population mean.
	It is sometimes stated that the "mean" means average. This is incorrect if "mean" is taken in the specific sense of "arithmetic mean" as there are different types of averages: the mean, median, and mode.
Wage	
	Several countries have enacted a statutory minimum Wage rate that sets a price floor for certain kinds of labor.
	Wage derives from words which suggest "making a promise," often in monetary form. Specifically from the Old French word wagier or gagier meaning to pledge or promise, from which the money placed in a bet also derives.
Household	The Household is "the basic residential unit in which economic production, consumption, inheritance, child rearing, and shelter are organized and carried out"; [the Household] "may or may not be synonymous with family".
	The Household is the basic unit of analysis in many social, microeconomic and government models. The term refers to all individuals who live in the same dwelling.

Permanent income hypothesis	The Permanent income hypothesis is a theory of consumption that was developed by the American economist Milton Friedman. In its simplest form, the hypothesis states that the choices made by consumers regarding their consumption patterns are determined not by current income but by their longer-term income expectations. The key conclusion of this theory is that transitory, short-term changes in income have little effect on consumer spending behavior.
Measure	The measures used in economics are physical measures, nominal price value measures and fixed price value measures. These measures differ from one another by the variables they measure and by the variables excluded from measurements. The measurable variables in economics are quantity, quality and distribution.
Human development index	The human development index is an index used to rank countries by level of "human development", which usually also implies whether a country is developed, developing, or underdeveloped.

The human development index combines normalized measures of life expectancy, educational attainment, and GDP per capita for countries worldwide. It is claimed as a standard means of measuring human development--a concept that, according to the United Nations Development Program (UNDP), refers to the process of widening the options of persons, giving them greater opportunities for education, health care, income, employment, etc. |
| Count | A Count is a nobleman in European Countries; his wife is a Countess. The word Count came into English from the French comte, itself from Latin comes--in its accusative comitem--meaning "companion", and later "companion of the emperor, delegate of the emperor". The British equivalent is an earl . |
| Relative deprivation | Relative deprivation is a situation in which a person is deprived of something which they think they are entitled to, while another person possesses it. The deprivation is relative between the two parties as a person possesses the item while the other does not.

The term can be used in social sciences to describe feelings or measures of economic, political, or social deprivation that are relative rather than absolute. |
Returns to scale	In economics, Returns to scale and economies of scale are related terms that describe what happens as the scale of production increases. They are different terms and should not be used interchangeably. .
Per capita Income	per capita income means how much each individual receives, in monetary terms, of the yearly income generated in the country. This is what each citizen is to receive if the yearly national income is divided equally among everyone. per capita income is usually reported in units of currency per year.
Asset	In business and accounting, Assets are economic resources owned by business or company. Anything tangible or intangible that one possesses, usually considered as applicable to the payment of one"s debts is considered an Asset. Simplistically stated, Assets are things of value that can be readily converted into cash (although cash itself is also considered an Asset).
Rural	Rural areas (referred to as "the countryside") are large and isolated areas of a country, often with low population density.

About 91 percent of the Rural population now earn salaried incomes, often in urban areas. The 10 percent who still produce resources generate 20 percent of the world"s coal, copper, and oil; 10 percent of its wheat, 20 percent of its meat, and 50 percent of its corn. |

Rural Poverty	Rural poverty refers to poverty found in rural areas, but more importantly, to factors of rural society, rural economy and rural political systems that give rise to the poverty found there. A widely shared assumption is that Rural poverty in the modern era operates on somewhat different dynamics than class-based urban poverty, although social science analyses since the "rediscovery " of poverty in the 1960s have often tended to conflate the two. Marxism, unlike other contemporary theories of poverty, tends to write off the rural problem without further examination.
Self-employment	Self-employment is where a person works for themselves rather than someone else or a company that they do not own. To be self-employed, an individual is normally highly skilled in a trade or has a niche product or service for their local community. With the creation of the Internet the ability for an individual to become self-employed has increased dramatically.
Employment	Employment is a contract between two parties, one being the employer and the other being the employee. An employee may be defined as: "A person in the service of another under any contract of hire, express or implied, oral or written, where the employer has the power or right to control and direct the employee in the material details of how the work is to be performed." Black"s Law Dictionary page 471 (5th ed. 1979).
	In a commercial setting, the employer conceives of a productive activity, generally with the intention of generating a profit, and the employee contributes labour to the enterprise, usually in return for payment of wages.
Informal sector	The Informal sector is economic activity that is neither taxed nor monitored by a government; and is not included in that government"s Gross National Product (GNP); as opposed to a formal economy.
	Although the informal economy is often associated with developing countries --where up to 60% of the labor force (with as much 40% of GDP) works, all economic systems contain an informal economy in some proportion. The term "Informal sector" was used in many earlier studies, and has been mostly replaced in more recent studies which use the newer term.
Unemployment	Unemployment occurs when a person is available to work and seeking work but currently without work. The prevalence of Unemployment is usually measured using the Unemployment rate, which is defined as the percentage of those in the labor force who are unemployed. The Unemployment rate is also used in economic studies and economic indices such as the United States" Conference Board"s Index of Leading Indicators as a measure of the state of the macroeconomics.
Trade	Trade is the voluntary exchange of goods, services, or both. Trade is also called commerce or transaction. A mechanism that allows Trade is called a market.
Bond market	The Bond market is a financial market where participants buy and sell debt securities, usually in the form of bonds. As of 2008, the size of the international Bond market is an estimated $67.0 trillion , of which the size of the outstanding U.S. Bond market debt was $33.5 trillion.
	Nearly all of the $923 billion average daily trading volume (as of early 2007) in the U.S. Bond market takes place between broker-dealers and large institutions in a decentralized, over-the-counter (OTC) market.
Loan	A Loan is a type of debt. Like all debt instruments, a Loan entails the redistribution of financial assets over time, between the lender and the borrower.

In a Loan, the borrower initially receives or borrows an amount of money, called the principal, from the lender, and is obligated to pay back or repay an equal amount of money to the lender at a later time.

Marginal utility

In economics, the Marginal utility of a good or of a service is the utility of the specific use to which an agent would put a given increase in that good or service, Marginal utility is the utility of the marginal use -- which, on the assumption of economic rationality, would be the least urgent use of the good or service, from the best feasible combination of actions in which its use is included. Under the mainstream assumptions, the Marginal utility of a good or service is the posited quantified change in utility obtained by increasing or by decreasing use of that good or service.

Incentive

In economics and sociology, an Incentive is any factor (financial or non-financial) that enables or motivates a particular course of action, the study of Incentive structures is central to the study of all economic activity (both in terms of individual decision-making and in terms of co-operation and competition within a larger institutional structure).

Insurance

Insurance, in law and economics, is a form of risk management primarily used to hedge against the risk of a contingent loss. Insurance is defined as the equitable transfer of the risk of a loss, from one entity to another, in exchange for a premium, and can be thought of as a guaranteed and known small loss to prevent a large, possibly devastating loss. An insurer is a company selling the Insurance; an insured or policyholder is the person or entity buying the Insurance.

Moral hazard

Moral hazard is the fact that a party insulated from risk may behave differently from the way it would behave if it would be fully exposed to the risk. In insurance, Moral hazard that occurs without conscious or malicious action is called morale hazard.

Moral hazard is a special case of information asymmetry, a situation in which one party in a transaction has more information than another.

Market access

market access for goods in the WTO means the conditions, tariff and non-tariff measures, agreed by members for the entry of specific goods into their markets. Tariff commitments for goods are set out in each member"s schedules of concessions on goods. The schedules represent commitments not to apply tariffs above the listed rates -- these rates are "bound".

Tenancy

Leasing is a process by which a firm can obtain the use of a certain fixed assets for which it must pay a series of contractual, periodic, tax deductible payments. The lessee is the receiver of the services or the assets under the lease contract and the lessor is the owner of the assets. The relationship between the tenant and the landlord is called a tenancy, and can be for a fixed or an indefinite period of time (called the term of the lease).

Energy balance

Energy balance has the following meanings in several fields:

· Energy Economics
· Energy Journal
· Resource and Energy Economics

There are several other journals that regularly publish papers in energy economics:

· Energy -- The International Journal
· Energy Policy
· International Journal of Global Energy Issues
· Utilities Policy

There is also a handbook in three volumes.

Much progress in energy economics has been made through the model comparison exercises of the (Stanford) Energy Modeling Forum and the meetings of the International Energy Workshop.

IDEAS/RePEc has a list of energy economists and a ranking of the same.

Reference man	The standard person or reference person is a theoretical individual that has perfectly "normal" characteristics. This model is used for much research into radiation safety. For many years, the standard person was called Reference man because the work assumed a healthy, young adult male.
Labor supply	In mainstream economic theories, the Labor supply is the number of total hours that workers wish to work at a given real wage rate. Realistically, the Labor supply is a function of various factors within an economy. For instance, overpopulation increases the number of available workers driving down wages and can result in high unemployment.
Supply and demand	Supply and demand is an economic model based on price, utility and quantity in a market. It concludes that in a competitive market, price will function to equalize the quantity demanded by consumers, and the quantity supplied by producers, resulting in an economic equilibrium of price and quantity. The demand schedule, depicted graphically as the demand curve, represents the amount of goods that buyers are willing and able to purchase at various prices, assuming all other non-price factors remain the same.
Pareto efficiency	Pareto efficiency, is an important concept in economics with broad applications in game theory, engineering and the social sciences. The term is named after Vilfredo Pareto, an Italian economist who used the concept in his studies of economic efficiency and income distribution. Informally, Pareto efficient situations are those in which any change to make any person better off is impossible without making someone else worse off.
Domestic worker	A domestic worker is someone who works within the employer"s household. domestic workers perform a variety of household services for an individual or a family, from providing care for children and elderly dependents to cleaning and household maintenance, known as housekeeping. Responsibilities may also include cooking, doing laundry and ironing, food shopping and other household errands.
Slavery	Slavery is a form of forced labor in which people are considered to be the property of others. Slaves can be held against their will from the time of their capture, purchase or birth, and deprived of the right to leave, to refuse to work, or to receive compensation (such as wages). Evidence of Slavery predates written records, and has existed to varying extents, forms and periods in almost all cultures and continents.
Productivity	Productivity is a measure of output from a production process, per unit of input. For example, lab is typically measured as a ratio of output per labor-hour, an input. Productivity may be conceived of as a metric of the technical or engineering efficiency of production.

Sharing	Sharing is the joint use of a resource or space. In its narrow sense, it refers to joint or alternating use of an inherently finite good, such as a common pasture or a shared residence. It is also the process of dividing and distributing.
Dot-com bubble	The "Dot-com bubble" (or) was a speculative bubble covering roughly 1998-2001 (with a climax on March 10, 2000 with the NASDAQ peaking at 5132.52) during which stock markets in Western nations saw their equity value rise rapidly from growth in the more recent Internet sector and related fields. While the latter part was a boom and bust cycle, the Internet boom sometimes is meant to refer to the steady commercial growth of the Internet with the advent of the world wide web as exemplified by the first release of the Mosaic web browser in 1993 and continuing through the 1990s. The period was marked by the founding (and, in many cases, spectacular failure) of a group of new Internet-based companies commonly referred to as dot-coms.
Widowhood	A widow is a woman whose spouse has died. A man whose spouse has died is a widower. The state of having lost one"s spouse to death is termed Widowhood or (occasionally) viduity.
General Agreement on Tariffs and Trade	The General Agreement on Tariffs and Trade was the outcome of the failure of negotiating governments to create the International Trade Organization (ITO). GATT was formed in 1947 and lasted until 1994, when it was replaced by the World Trade Organization in 1995. The Bretton Woods Conference had introduced the idea for an organization to regulate trade as part of a larger plan for economic recovery after World War II. As governments negotiated the ITO, 15 negotiating states began parallel negotiations for the GATT as a way to attain early tariff reductions. Once the ITO failed in 1950, only the GATT agreement was left.
Nominative determinism	Nominative determinism refers to the theory that a person"s name is given an influential role in reflecting key attributes of his job, profession, but real examples are more highly prized, the more obscure the better.
Information	Information as a concept has many meanings, from everyday usage to technical settings. The concept of Information is closely related to notions of constraint, communication, control, data, form, instruction, knowledge, meaning, mental stimulus, pattern, perception, and representation. The English word was apparently derived from the Latin accusative form of the nominative (informatio): this noun is in its turn derived from the verb "informare" (to inform) in the sense of "to give form to the mind", "to discipline", "instruct", "teach": "Men so wise should go and inform their kings." (1330) Inform itself comes from the Latin verb informare, to give form to, to form an idea of.

Exponential growth	Exponential growth (including exponential decay) occurs when the growth rate of a mathematical function is proportional to the function"s current value. In the case of a discrete domain of definition with equal intervals it is also called geometric growth or geometric decay (the function values form a geometric progression).
	The Exponential growth model is also known as the Malthusian growth model.
Distribution	Distribution in economics refers to the way total output or income is distributed among individuals or among the factors of production (labor, land, and capital) (Samuelson and Nordhaus, 2001, p. 762). In general theory and the national income and product accounts, each unit of output corresponds to a unit of income. One use of national accounts is for classifying factor incomes and measuring their respective shares, as in National Income.
Anecdotal value	In economics, Anecdotal value refers to the primarily social and political value of an anecdote or anecdotal evidence in promoting understanding of a social, cultural, in the last several decades the evaluation of anecdotes has received sustained academic scrutiny from economists and scholars such as S.G. Checkland (on David Ricardo), Steven Novella, Hollis Robbins, R. Charleton, Kwamena Kwansah-Aidoo, and others; these academics seek to quantify the value inherent in the deployment of anecdotes. More recently, economists studying choice models have begun assessing Anecdotal value in the context of framing; Kahneman and Tversky suggest that choice models may be contingent on stories or anecdotes that frame or influence choice.
Third World	The term Third World arose during the Cold War to define countries that remained non-aligned or neutral with either capitalism and NATO (which along with its allies represented the First World) or communism and the Soviet Union (which along with its allies represented the Second World). This definition provided a way of broadly categorizing the nations of the Earth into three groups based on social, political, and economic divisions. Although the term continues to be used colloquially to describe the poorest countries in the world, this usage is widely disparaged since the term no longer holds any verifiable meaning after the fall of the Soviet Union deprecated the terms First World and Second World.
Total-factor productivity	In economics, total-factor productivity (TFP) is a variable which accounts for effects in total output not caused by inputs. For example, a year with unusually good weather will tend to have higher output, because bad weather hinders agricultural output. A variable like weather does not directly relate to unit inputs, so weather is considered a total-factor productivity variable.
Demographic	Demographics data refers to selected population characteristics as used in government, marketing or opinion research). Commonly-used Demographics include race, age, income, disabilities, mobility (in terms of travel time to work or number of vehicles available), educational attainment, home ownership, employment status, and even location.
Factor	A factor or limiting resource is a factor that controls a process, such as organism growth or species population, size, or distribution. The availability of food, predation pressure, or availability of shelter are examples of factors that could be limiting for an organism. An example of a limiting factor is sunlight, which is crucial in rainforests.
Birth rate	Crude Birth rate is the nativity or childbirths per 1,000 people per year.
	According to the United Nations" World Population Prospects: The 2008 Revision Population Database, crude Birth rate is the Number of births over a given period divided by the person-years lived by the population over that period. It is expressed as number of births per 1,000 population.

Population growth rate	Population growth is the change in population over time, and can be quantified as the change in the number of individuals in a population using "per unit time" for measurement. The term population growth can technically refer to any species, but almost always refers to humans, and it is often used informally for the more specific demographic term Population growth rate , and is often used to refer specifically to the growth of the population of the world.
	Simple models of population growth include the Malthusian Growth Model and the logistic model.
Per capita Income	per capita income means how much each individual receives, in monetary terms, of the yearly income generated in the country. This is what each citizen is to receive if the yearly national income is divided equally among everyone. per capita income is usually reported in units of currency per year.
Total fertility rate	The Total fertility rate of a population is the average number of children that would be born to a woman over her lifetime if (1) she were to experience the exact current age-specific fertility rates (ASFRs) through her lifetime, and (2) she were to survive from birth through the end of her reproductive life. It is obtained by summing the single-year age-specific rates at a given time.
	The Total fertility rate is a synthetic rate, not something that is actually counted.
Demographic transition	The Demographic transition model (DTM) is a model used to represent the process of explaining the transformation of countries from high birth rates and high death rates to low birth rates and low death rates as part of the economic development of a country from a pre-industrial to an industrialized economy. It is based on an interpretation begun in 1929 by the American demographer Warren Thompson of prior observed changes, or transitions, in birth and death rates in industrialized societies over the past two hundred years.
	Most developed countries are beyond stage three of the model; the majority of developing countries are in stage 2 or stage 3. The model was based on the changes seen in Europe so these countries follow the DTM relatively well.
Productivity	Productivity is a measure of output from a production process, per unit of input. For example, lab is typically measured as a ratio of output per labor-hour, an input. Productivity may be conceived of as a metric of the technical or engineering efficiency of production.
Cooperation	Distinguish from Corporation.
	Cooperation, co-operation, or coöperation is the process of working or acting together, which can be accomplished by both intentional and non-intentional agents. In its simplest form it involves things working in harmony, side by side, while in its more complicated forms, it can involve something as complex as the inner workings of a human being or even the social patterns of a nation.
Insurance	Insurance, in law and economics, is a form of risk management primarily used to hedge against the risk of a contingent loss. Insurance is defined as the equitable transfer of the risk of a loss, from one entity to another, in exchange for a premium, and can be thought of as a guaranteed and known small loss to prevent a large, possibly devastating loss. An insurer is a company selling the Insurance; an insured or policyholder is the person or entity buying the Insurance.
Organisation for Economic Co-operation and Development	The Organisation for Economic Co-operation and Development (OECD) is an international organisation of 30 countries that accept the principles of representative democracy and free-market economy. Most OECD members are high-income economies with a high HDI and are regarded as developed countries.

It originated in 1948 as the Organisation for European Economic Co-operation , led by Robert Marjolin of France, to help administer the Marshall Plan for the reconstruction of Europe after World War II. Later, its membership was extended to non-European states.

Retirement	Retirement is the point where a person stops employment completely (or decides to leave the labor force if he or she is unemployed). A person may also semi-retire by reducing work hours. Many people choose to retire when they are eligible for private or public pension benefits, although some are forced to retire when physical conditions don"t allow the person to work any more (by illness or accident).
Disability Insurance	Disability insurance, often called disability income insurance, is a form of insurance that insures the beneficiary"s earned income against the risk that disability will make working (and therefore earning) impossible. It includes paid sick leave, short-term disability benefits, and long-term disability benefits. In most developed countries, the single most important form of Disability insurance is that provided by the national government for all citizens.
Missing market	A Missing market is a situation in microeconomics where a competitive market allowing the exchange of a commodity would be Pareto-efficient, but no such market exists. A variety of factors can lead to Missing markets: A classic example of a Missing market is the case of an externality like pollution, where decision makers are not responsible for some of the consequences of their actions. When a factory discharges polluted water into a river, that pollution can hurt people who fish in or get their drinking water from the river downstream, but the factory owner may have no incentive to consider those consequences.
Asset	In business and accounting, Assets are economic resources owned by business or company. Anything tangible or intangible that one possesses, usually considered as applicable to the payment of one"s debts is considered an Asset. Simplistically stated, Assets are things of value that can be readily converted into cash (although cash itself is also considered an Asset).
General Agreement on Tariffs and Trade	The General Agreement on Tariffs and Trade was the outcome of the failure of negotiating governments to create the International Trade Organization (ITO). GATT was formed in 1947 and lasted until 1994, when it was replaced by the World Trade Organization in 1995. The Bretton Woods Conference had introduced the idea for an organization to regulate trade as part of a larger plan for economic recovery after World War II. As governments negotiated the ITO, 15 negotiating states began parallel negotiations for the GATT as a way to attain early tariff reductions. Once the ITO failed in 1950, only the GATT agreement was left.
Nominative determinism	Nominative determinism refers to the theory that a person"s name is given an influential role in reflecting key attributes of his job, profession, but real examples are more highly prized, the more obscure the better.
Trade	Trade is the voluntary exchange of goods, services, or both. Trade is also called commerce or transaction. A mechanism that allows Trade is called a market.
Hoarding	Hoarding is a general term for the accumulation of food or other items. The term is used to describe both animal and human behavior.

Hoarding of food is a natural behaviour in certain species of animals. Such Hoarding occurs in two forms:

· Larder Hoarding, the collection of large amounts of food in a single place (a larder), which usually also serves as the nest where the animal lives.

Cost

In business, retail, and accounting, a cost is the value of money that has been used up to produce something, and hence is not available for use anymore. In economics, a cost is an alternative that is given up as a result of a decision. In business, the cost may be one of acquisition, in which case the amount of money expended to acquire it is counted as cost.

Direct costs

Direct costs are those costs for activities or services that benefit specific projects, e.g., salaries for project staff and materials required for a particular project. Because these activities are easily traced to projects, their costs are usually charged to projects on an item-by-item basis.

Reduced cost

In linear programming, Reduced cost, is the amount by which an objective function would have to improve (so increase for maximization problem, decrease for minimization problem) before it would be possible for a corresponding variable to assume a positive value in the optimal solution. It is cost for increasing a variable by a small amount, i.e., the first derivative from a certain point on the polyhedron that constraints the problem. When the point is a vertex in the polyhedron, the variable with the most extreme cost, negatively for minimisation and positively maximisation, is sometimes referred to as the steepest edge.

Wage

Several countries have enacted a statutory minimum Wage rate that sets a price floor for certain kinds of labor. Wage derives from words which suggest "making a promise," often in monetary form. Specifically from the Old French word wagier or gagier meaning to pledge or promise, from which the money placed in a bet also derives.

Wage rate

Several countries have enacted a statutory minimum wage rate that sets a price floor for certain kinds of labor. Wage derives from words which suggest "making a promise," often in monetary form. Specifically from the Old French word wagier or gagier meaning to pledge or promise, from which the money placed in a bet also derives.

Cost-benefit

cost-benefit analysis is a term that refers both to:

· helping to appraise, or assess, the case for a project or proposal, which itself is a process known as project appraisal; and
· an informal approach to making decisions of any kind.
Under both definitions the process involves, whether explicitly or implicitly, weighing the total expected costs against the total expected benefits of one or more actions in order to choose the best or most profitable option. The formal process is often referred to as either CBA (cost-benefit Analysis) or BCA (Benefit-Cost Analysis).

Information

Information as a concept has many meanings, from everyday usage to technical settings. The concept of Information is closely related to notions of constraint, communication, control, data, form, instruction, knowledge, meaning, mental stimulus, pattern, perception, and representation.

	The English word was apparently derived from the Latin accusative form of the nominative (informatio): this noun is in its turn derived from the verb "informare" (to inform) in the sense of "to give form to the mind", "to discipline", "instruct", "teach": "Men so wise should go and inform their kings." (1330) Inform itself comes from the Latin verb informare, to give form to, to form an idea of.
Social cost	In neoclassical economics social cost is defined as the sum of private and external costs. Neoclassical economic theorists ascribe individual decision-making to a calculation costs and benefits. Rational choice theory assumes that individuals only consider their own private costs when making decisions, not the costs that may be borne by others.
Conformism	Conformism is a term used to describe the suspension of an individual"s self-determined actions or opinions in favour of obedience to the mandates or conventions of one"s peer-group
Production	Production refers to the economic process of converting of inputs into outputs and is a field of study in microeconomics. Production uses resources to create a good or service that is suitable for exchange. This can include manufacturing, storing, shipping, and packaging.
Production function	In economics, a Production function is a function that specifies the output of a firm, an industry) compares the practice of the existing entities converting inputs X into output y to determine the most efficient practice Production function of the existing entities, whether the most efficient feasible practice production or the most efficient actual practice production. In either case, the maximum output of a technologically-determined production process is a mathematical function of input factors of production.
Steady state	A system in a Steady state has numerous properties that are unchanging in time. The concept of Steady state has relevance in many fields, in particular thermodynamics. Steady state is a more general situation than dynamic equilibrium.
Diminishing returns	In economics, Diminishing returns refers to how the marginal production of a factor of production, in contrast to the increase that would otherwise be normally expected, actually starts to progressively decrease the more of the factor are added. According to this relationship, in a production system with fixed and variable inputs (say factory size and labor), beyond some point, each additional unit of the variable input (IE man*hours) yields smaller and smaller increases in outputs, also reducing the mean productivity of each worker. Conversely, producing one more unit of output, costs more and more (due to the major amount of variable inputs being used,to little effect) This concept is also known as the law of diminishing marginal returns or the law of increasing relative cost.
Labor force	In economics, the people in the Labor force are the suppliers of labor. The Labor force is all the nonmilitary people who are employed or unemployed. In 2005, the worldwide Labor force was over 3 billion people.
Marginal product	In economics, the Marginal product or marginal physical product is the extra output produced by one more unit of an input . Assuming that no other inputs to production change, the Marginal product of a given input (X) can be expressed as: Marginal product = $\Delta Y / \Delta X$ = (the change of Y)/(the change of X). In neoclassical economics, this is the mathematical derivative of the production function....

| Demand | In economics, demand is the desire to own anything and the ability to pay for it. . The term demand signifies the ability or the willingness to buy a particular commodity at a given point of time. |

Labor supply	In mainstream economic theories, the Labor supply is the number of total hours that workers wish to work at a given real wage rate. Realistically, the Labor supply is a function of various factors within an economy. For instance, overpopulation increases the number of available workers driving down wages and can result in high unemployment.
Rural	Rural areas (referred to as "the countryside") are large and isolated areas of a country, often with low population density.
	About 91 percent of the Rural population now earn salaried incomes, often in urban areas. The 10 percent who still produce resources generate 20 percent of the world"s coal, copper, and oil; 10 percent of its wheat, 20 percent of its meat, and 50 percent of its corn.
Informal Sector	The Informal sector is economic activity that is neither taxed nor monitored by a government; and is not included in that government"s Gross National Product (GNP); as opposed to a formal economy.
	Although the informal economy is often associated with developing countries --where up to 60% of the labor force (with as much 40% of GDP) works, all economic systems contain an informal economy in some proportion. The term "Informal sector" was used in many earlier studies, and has been mostly replaced in more recent studies which use the newer term.
High-yielding varieties	High-yielding varieties (HYVs) are any of a group of genetically enhanced cultivars of crops such as rice, maize and wheat that have an increased growth rate, an increased percentage of usable plant parts or an increased resistance against crop diseases. Those crops formed the basis for the Green Revolution. In general, they require a higher level of agricultural care, such as intensive disease control, higher fertilizer levels and controlled water supply.
Dual economy	A Dual economy is the existence of two separate economic systems within one country. Dual economies are common in less developed countries, where one system is geared to local needs and another to the global export market.
	Dual economies need not be across economic sector boundaries.
Labor force	In economics, the people in the Labor force are the suppliers of labor. The Labor force is all the nonmilitary people who are employed or unemployed. In 2005, the worldwide Labor force was over 3 billion people.
Self-sufficiency	Self-sufficiency refers to the state of not requiring any outside aid, support, for survival; it is therefore a type of personal or collective autonomy. On a large scale, a totally self-sufficient economy that does not trade with the outside world is called an autarky.
	The term Self-sufficiency is usually applied to varieties of sustainable living in which nothing is consumed outside of what is produced by the self-sufficient individuals.
Capital market	A Capital market is a market for securities (both debt and equity), where business enterprises (companies) and governments can raise long-term funds. It is defined as a market in which money is lent for periods longer than a year, as the raising of short-term funds takes place on other markets (e.g., the money market). The Capital market includes the stock market (equity securities) and the bond market (debt).
Industry	An industry is the manufacturing of a good or service within a category. Although industry is a broad term for any kind of economic production, in economics and urban planning industry is a synonym for the secondary sector, which is a type of economic activity involved in the manufacturing of raw materials into goods and products.

87

There are four key industrial economic sectors: the primary sector, largely raw material extraction industries such as mining and farming; the secondary sector, involving refining, construction, and manufacturing; the tertiary sector, which deals with services and distribution of manufactured goods; and the quaternary sector, a relatively new type of knowledge industry focusing on technological research, design and development such as computer programming, and biochemistry.

Reduced cost

In linear programming, Reduced cost, is the amount by which an objective function would have to improve (so increase for maximization problem, decrease for minimization problem) before it would be possible for a corresponding variable to assume a positive value in the optimal solution. It is cost for increasing a variable by a small amount, i.e., the first derivative from a certain point on the polyhedron that constraints the problem. When the point is a vertex in the polyhedron, the variable with the most extreme cost, negatively for minimisation and positively maximisation, is sometimes referred to as the steepest edge.

Marginal product

In economics, the Marginal product or marginal physical product is the extra output produced by one more unit of an input . Assuming that no other inputs to production change, the Marginal product of a given input (X) can be expressed as:

Marginal product = $\Delta Y/\Delta X$ = (the change of Y)/(the change of X).

In neoclassical economics, this is the mathematical derivative of the production function....

Production

Production refers to the economic process of converting of inputs into outputs and is a field of study in microeconomics. Production uses resources to create a good or service that is suitable for exchange. This can include manufacturing, storing, shipping, and packaging.

Production function

In economics, a Production function is a function that specifies the output of a firm, an industry) compares the practice of the existing entities converting inputs X into output y to determine the most efficient practice Production function of the existing entities, whether the most efficient feasible practice production or the most efficient actual practice production. In either case, the maximum output of a technologically-determined production process is a mathematical function of input factors of production.

Wage

Several countries have enacted a statutory minimum Wage rate that sets a price floor for certain kinds of labor.

Wage derives from words which suggest "making a promise," often in monetary form. Specifically from the Old French word wagier or gagier meaning to pledge or promise, from which the money placed in a bet also derives.

Sharing

Sharing is the joint use of a resource or space. In its narrow sense, it refers to joint or alternating use of an inherently finite good, such as a common pasture or a shared residence. It is also the process of dividing and distributing.

Round robin test

In experimental methodology, a Round robin test is a test (measurement, analysis) performed independently several times. This can involve multiple independent scientists performing the test with the use of the same method in different equipment, or a variety of methods and equipment. In reality it is often a combination of the two, for example if a sample is analysed, or one (or more) of its properties is measured by different laboratories using different methods, or even just by different units of equipment of identical construction.

There are different reasons for performing a Round robin test:

· Verification of a new method of analysis: If a new method of analysis has been developed, a Round robin test involving proven methods would verify whether the new method produces results that agree with the established method

Unemployment

Unemployment occurs when a person is available to work and seeking work but currently without work. The prevalence of Unemployment is usually measured using the Unemployment rate, which is defined as the percentage of those in the labor force who are unemployed. The Unemployment rate is also used in economic studies and economic indices such as the United States" Conference Board"s Index of Leading Indicators as a measure of the state of the macroeconomics.

Laborers

One of the construction trades, traditionally considered unskilled manual labor (as opposed to skilled labor). In the division of labor, Laborers have all blasting, hand tools, power tools, air tools, and small heavy equipment, and act as assistants to other trades , e.g. operators or cement masons. The first century BC engineer Vitruvius writes in detail about laborer practices at that time.

Marginal cost

In economics and finance, Marginal cost is the change in total cost that arises when the quantity produced changes by one unit. It is the cost of producing one more unit of a good. Mathematically, the Marginal cost function is expressed as the first derivative of the total cost (TC) function with respect to quantity (Q).

Mean

In statistics, mean has two related meanings:

· the arithmetic mean .
· the expected value of a random variable, which is also called the population mean.
It is sometimes stated that the "mean" means average. This is incorrect if "mean" is taken in the specific sense of "arithmetic mean" as there are different types of averages: the mean, median, and mode.

Wage rate

Several countries have enacted a statutory minimum wage rate that sets a price floor for certain kinds of labor.
Wage derives from words which suggest "making a promise," often in monetary form. Specifically from the Old French word wagier or gagier meaning to pledge or promise, from which the money placed in a bet also derives.

Commercialization

Commercialization is the process or cycle of introducing a new product into the market. The actual launch of a new product is the final stage of new product development, and the one where the most money will have to be spent for advertising, sales promotion, and other marketing efforts. In the case of a new consumer packaged good, costs will be at least $ 10 million, but can reach up to $ 200 million.

Demand

In economics, demand is the desire to own anything and the ability to pay for it. . The term demand signifies the ability or the willingness to buy a particular commodity at a given point of time.

Dot-com bubble

The "Dot-com bubble" (or) was a speculative bubble covering roughly 1998-2001 (with a climax on March 10, 2000 with the NASDAQ peaking at 5132.52) during which stock markets in Western nations saw their equity value rise rapidly from growth in the more recent Internet sector and related fields. While the latter part was a boom and bust cycle, the Internet boom sometimes is meant to refer to the steady commercial growth of the Internet with the advent of the world wide web as exemplified by the first release of the Mosaic web browser in 1993 and continuing through the 1990s.

The period was marked by the founding (and, in many cases, spectacular failure) of a group of new Internet-based companies commonly referred to as dot-coms.

Pricing	Pricing is a fundamental aspect of financial modelling, and is one of the four Ps of the marketing mix. The other three aspects are product, promotion, and place. It is also a key variable in microeconomic price allocation theory. Price is the only revenue generating element amongst the four Ps, the rest being cost centers. Pricing is the manual or automatic process of applying prices to purchase and sales orders, based on factors such as: a fixed amount, quantity break, promotion or sales campaign, specific vendor quote, price prevailing on entry, shipment or invoice date, combination of multiple orders or lines, and many others.
Balance of payments	In economics, the Balance of payments, measures the payments that flow between any individual country and all other countries. It is used to summarize all international economic transactions for that country during a specific time period, usually a year. The Balance of payments is determined by the country"s exports and imports of goods, services, and financial capital, as well as financial transfers.
Price	price in economics and business is the result of an exchange and from that trade we assign a numerical monetary value to a good, service or asset. If Alice trades Bob 4 apples for an orange, the price of an orange is 4 apples. Inversely, the price of an apple is 1/4 oranges.
Structural adjustment	Structural adjustment is a term used to describe the policy changes implemented by the International Monetary Fund (IMF) and the World Bank (the Bretton Woods Institutions) in developing countries. These policy changes are conditions (Conditionalities) for getting new loans from the IMF or World Bank, or for obtaining lower interest rates on existing loans. Conditionalities are implemented to ensure that the money lent will be spent in accordance with the overall goals of the loan.
Structural adjustment loan	Structural adjustment loan is a type of loan to developing countries. They are one of the economic tools supported by the World Bank for structural adjustment. They carry policy conditionalities such as currency devaluation (to stimulate the supply of exports); the conversion of import quotas into import tariffs to reduce rent-seeking (and then tariff reduction in order to place more competitive pressure on inefficient infant industries); the removal (liberalization) of market controls in agriculture (to provide more incentives for farmers); and the reform of public expenditures and taxation (to shift more spending towards development priorities and to mobilize more public revenues to finance spending)..
Payment	A Payment is the transfer of wealth from one party (such as a person or company) to another. A Payment is usually made in exchange for the provision of goods, services or both, or to fulfill a legal obligation. The simplest and oldest form of Payment is barter, the exchange of one good or service for another.
Total-factor productivity	In economics, total-factor productivity (TFP) is a variable which accounts for effects in total output not caused by inputs. For example, a year with unusually good weather will tend to have higher output, because bad weather hinders agricultural output. A variable like weather does not directly relate to unit inputs, so weather is considered a total-factor productivity variable.

Factor	A factor or limiting resource is a factor that controls a process, such as organism growth or species population, size, or distribution. The availability of food, predation pressure, or availability of shelter are examples of factors that could be limiting for an organism. An example of a limiting factor is sunlight, which is crucial in rainforests.
Harris-Todaro model	The Harris-Todaro Model is an economic model used in development economics and welfare economics to explain some of the issues concerning rural-urban migration. The main result of the model is that the migration decision is based on expected income differentials between rural and urban areas, not wage differentials. This implies that rural-urban migration in a context of high urban unemployment can be economically rational if expected urban income exceeds expected rural income.
Profit maximization	In economics, Profit maximization is the process by which a firm determines the price and output level that returns the greatest profit. There are several approaches to this problem. The total revenue--total cost method relies on the fact that profit equals revenue minus cost, and the marginal revenue--marginal cost method is based on the fact that total profit in a perfectly competitive market reaches its maximum point where marginal revenue equals marginal cost.
Demand curve	In economics, the Demand curve can be defined as the graph depicting the relationship between the price of a certain commodity, and the amount of it that consumers are willing and able to purchase at that given price. It is a graphic representation of a demand schedule. The Demand curve for all consumers together follows from the Demand curve of every individual consumer: the individual demands at each price are added together.
Tax profit	Tax profit or taxable profit is used to distinguish between accounting profit or earnings (the number that is generally referred to in financial results for public companies and quoted in the press). Taxable profit is the number that is used to calculate profit tax.
	For a number of reasons, taxable profit may differ from reported earnings, and may be higher or lower.
Risk aversion	Risk aversion is a concept in economics, finance, and psychology related to the behaviour of consumers and investors under uncertainty. Risk aversion is the reluctance of a person to accept a bargain with an uncertain payoff rather than another bargain with a more certain, but possibly lower, expected payoff. For example, a risk-averse investor might choose to put his or her money into a bank account with a low but guaranteed interest rate, rather than into a stock that is likely to have high returns, but also has a chance of becoming worthless.
Utility	In economics, Utility is a measure of the relative satisfaction from or desirability of, consumption of various goods and services. Given this measure, one may speak meaningfully of increasing or decreasing Utility, and thereby explain economic behavior in terms of attempts to increase one"s Utility. For illustrative purposes, changes in Utility are sometimes expressed in fictional units called utils (fictional in that there is no standard scale for them).
Marginal utility	In economics, the Marginal utility of a good or of a service is the utility of the specific use to which an agent would put a given increase in that good or service, Marginal utility is the utility of the marginal use -- which, on the assumption of economic rationality, would be the least urgent use of the good or service, from the best feasible combination of actions in which its use is included. Under the mainstream assumptions, the Marginal utility of a good or service is the posited quantified change in utility obtained by increasing or by decreasing use of that good or service.

Expected Utility	In economics, game theory, and decision theory the Expected utility theorem predicts that the "betting preferences" of people with regard to uncertain outcomes (gambles) can be described by a mathematical relation which takes into account the size of a payout (whether in money or other goods), the probability of occurrence, risk aversion, and the different utility of the same payout to people with different assets or personal preferences. It is a more sophisticated theory than simply predicting that choices will be made based on expected value (which takes into account only the size of the payout and the probability of occurrence). Daniel Bernoulli described the complete theory in 1738. John von Neumann and Oskar Morgenstern reinterpreted and presented an axiomatization of the same theory in 1944. They proved that any "normal" preference relation over a finite set of states can be written as an Expected utility, sometimes referred to as von Neumann-Morgenstern utility.
Insurance	Insurance, in law and economics, is a form of risk management primarily used to hedge against the risk of a contingent loss. Insurance is defined as the equitable transfer of the risk of a loss, from one entity to another, in exchange for a premium, and can be thought of as a guaranteed and known small loss to prevent a large, possibly devastating loss. An insurer is a company selling the Insurance; an insured or policyholder is the person or entity buying the Insurance.
Multiple comparisons	In statistics, the Multiple comparisons (or "multiple testing") problem occurs when one considers a set, of statistical inferences simultaneously. Errors in inference, including confidence intervals that fail to include their corresponding population parameters, or hypothesis tests that incorrectly reject the null hypothesis, are more likely to occur when one considers the family as a whole. Several statistical techniques have been developed to prevent this from happening, allowing significance levels for single and Multiple comparisons to be directly compared.

Missing market	A Missing market is a situation in microeconomics where a competitive market allowing the exchange of a commodity would be Pareto-efficient, but no such market exists. A variety of factors can lead to Missing markets: A classic example of a Missing market is the case of an externality like pollution, where decision makers are not responsible for some of the consequences of their actions. When a factory discharges polluted water into a river, that pollution can hurt people who fish in or get their drinking water from the river downstream, but the factory owner may have no incentive to consider those consequences.
Incentive	In economics and sociology, an Incentive is any factor (financial or non-financial) that enables or motivates a particular course of action, the study of Incentive structures is central to the study of all economic activity (both in terms of individual decision-making and in terms of co-operation and competition within a larger institutional structure).
Moral hazard	Moral hazard is the fact that a party insulated from risk may behave differently from the way it would behave if it would be fully exposed to the risk. In insurance, Moral hazard that occurs without conscious or malicious action is called morale hazard. Moral hazard is a special case of information asymmetry, a situation in which one party in a transaction has more information than another.
Information	Information as a concept has many meanings, from everyday usage to technical settings. The concept of Information is closely related to notions of constraint, communication, control, data, form, instruction, knowledge, meaning, mental stimulus, pattern, perception, and representation. The English word was apparently derived from the Latin accusative form of the nominative (informatio): this noun is in its turn derived from the verb "informare" (to inform) in the sense of "to give form to the mind", "to discipline", "instruct", "teach": "Men so wise should go and inform their kings." (1330) Inform itself comes from the Latin verb informare, to give form to, to form an idea of.
Insurance	Insurance, in law and economics, is a form of risk management primarily used to hedge against the risk of a contingent loss. Insurance is defined as the equitable transfer of the risk of a loss, from one entity to another, in exchange for a premium, and can be thought of as a guaranteed and known small loss to prevent a large, possibly devastating loss. An insurer is a company selling the Insurance; an insured or policyholder is the person or entity buying the Insurance.
Limited liability	Limited liability is a concept whereby a person"s financial liability is limited to a fixed sum, most commonly the value of a person"s investment in a company or partnership with Limited liability. In other words, if a company with Limited liability is sued, then the plaintiffs are suing the company, not its owners or investors. A shareholder in a limited company is not personally liable for any of the debts of the company, other than for the value of his investment in that company.
Rationing	Rationing is the controlled distribution of resources and scarce goods or services. Rationing controls the size of the ration, one"s allotted portion of the resources being distributed on a particular day or at a particular time. In economics, it is often common to use the word "Rationing" to refer to one of the roles that prices play in markets, while Rationing (as the word is usually used) is called "non-price Rationing".

Africa	Africa has a large quantity of natural resources including oil, diamonds, gold, cobalt, uranium, copper, bauxite, but also woods and tropical fruits. Having a low human density, for a long period of time Africa has been colonized by more dynamic groups, exploiting African resources. Some economists have talked about the "scurge of raw materials", large quantities of rare raw materials putting Africa under heavy pressures and tensions, leading to wars and slow development.
Rural	Rural areas (referred to as "the countryside") are large and isolated areas of a country, often with low population density. About 91 percent of the Rural population now earn salaried incomes, often in urban areas. The 10 percent who still produce resources generate 20 percent of the world"s coal, copper, and oil; 10 percent of its wheat, 20 percent of its meat, and 50 percent of its corn.
Slavery	Slavery is a form of forced labor in which people are considered to be the property of others. Slaves can be held against their will from the time of their capture, purchase or birth, and deprived of the right to leave, to refuse to work, or to receive compensation (such as wages). Evidence of Slavery predates written records, and has existed to varying extents, forms and periods in almost all cultures and continents.
Productivity	Productivity is a measure of output from a production process, per unit of input. For example, lab is typically measured as a ratio of output per labor-hour, an input. Productivity may be conceived of as a metric of the technical or engineering efficiency of production.
Distribution	Distribution in economics refers to the way total output or income is distributed among individuals or among the factors of production (labor, land, and capital) (Samuelson and Nordhaus, 2001, p. 762). In general theory and the national income and product accounts, each unit of output corresponds to a unit of income. One use of national accounts is for classifying factor incomes and measuring their respective shares, as in National Income.
Tenancy	Leasing is a process by which a firm can obtain the use of a certain fixed assets for which it must pay a series of contractual, periodic, tax deductible payments. The lessee is the receiver of the services or the assets under the lease contract and the lessor is the owner of the assets. The relationship between the tenant and the landlord is called a tenancy, and can be for a fixed or an indefinite period of time (called the term of the lease).
Personal property	Personal property is a type of property. In the common law systems Personal property may also be called chattels. It is distinguished from real property, or real estate.
Bond market	The Bond market is a financial market where participants buy and sell debt securities, usually in the form of bonds. As of 2008, the size of the international Bond market is an estimated $67.0 trillion , of which the size of the outstanding U.S. Bond market debt was $33.5 trillion. Nearly all of the $923 billion average daily trading volume (as of early 2007) in the U.S. Bond market takes place between broker-dealers and large institutions in a decentralized, over-the-counter (OTC) market.

Distribution	Distribution in economics refers to the way total output or income is distributed among individuals or among the factors of production (labor, land, and capital) (Samuelson and Nordhaus, 2001, p. 762). In general theory and the national income and product accounts, each unit of output corresponds to a unit of income. One use of national accounts is for classifying factor incomes and measuring their respective shares, as in National Income.
Productivity	Productivity is a measure of output from a production process, per unit of input. For example, lab is typically measured as a ratio of output per labor-hour, an input. Productivity may be conceived of as a metric of the technical or engineering efficiency of production.
Anecdotal value	In economics, Anecdotal value refers to the primarily social and political value of an anecdote or anecdotal evidence in promoting understanding of a social, cultural, in the last several decades the evaluation of anecdotes has received sustained academic scrutiny from economists and scholars such as S.G. Checkland (on David Ricardo), Steven Novella, Hollis Robbins, R. Charleton, Kwamena Kwansah-Aidoo, and others; these academics seek to quantify the value inherent in the deployment of anecdotes. More recently, economists studying choice models have begun assessing Anecdotal value in the context of framing; Kahneman and Tversky suggest that choice models may be contingent on stories or anecdotes that frame or influence choice.
Economic efficiency	Economic efficiency is used to refer to a number of related concepts. It is the using of resources in such a way as to maximize the production of goods and services. A system can be called economically efficient if: · No one can be made better off without making someone else worse off. · More output cannot be obtained without increasing the amount of inputs. · Production proceeds at the lowest possible per-unit cost. These definitions of efficiency are not equivalent, but they are all encompassed by the idea that nothing more can be achieved given the resources available.
Income distribution	In economics, the Lorenz curve is a graphical representation of the cumulative distribution function of a probability distribution; it is a graph showing the proportion of the distribution assumed by the bottom y% of the values. It is often used to represent income Distribution, where it shows for the bottom x% of households, what percentage y% of the total income they have. The percentage of households is plotted on the x-axis, the percentage of income on the y-axis.
Personal property	Personal property is a type of property. In the common law systems Personal property may also be called chattels. It is distinguished from real property, or real estate.
Tenancy	Leasing is a process by which a firm can obtain the use of a certain fixed assets for which it must pay a series of contractual, periodic, tax deductible payments. The lessee is the receiver of the services or the assets under the lease contract and the lessor is the owner of the assets. The relationship between the tenant and the landlord is called a tenancy, and can be for a fixed or an indefinite period of time (called the term of the lease).
Rights	rights are entitlements or permissions, usually of a legal or moral nature. rights are of vital importance in the fields of law and ethics, especially theories of justice and deontology. There are numerous different theoretical distinctions in accordance with which rights may be classified.

Share	In financial markets, a Share is a unit of account for various financial instruments including stocks (ordinary or preferential), and investments in limited partnerships, and REITs. The common feature of all these is equity participation (limited in the case of preference Shares). In American English, the plural stocks is widely used instead of Shares, in other words to refer to the stock (or perhaps originally stock certificates) of even a single company.
Dot-com bubble	The "Dot-com bubble" (or) was a speculative bubble covering roughly 1998-2001 (with a climax on March 10, 2000 with the NASDAQ peaking at 5132.52) during which stock markets in Western nations saw their equity value rise rapidly from growth in the more recent Internet sector and related fields. While the latter part was a boom and bust cycle, the Internet boom sometimes is meant to refer to the steady commercial growth of the Internet with the advent of the world wide web as exemplified by the first release of the Mosaic web browser in 1993 and continuing through the 1990s. The period was marked by the founding (and, in many cases, spectacular failure) of a group of new Internet-based companies commonly referred to as dot-coms.
Landed property	Landed property or landed estates is a real estate term that usually refers to a property that generates income for the owner without the owner having to do the actual work of the estate. In Europe, agrarian Landed property typically consisted of a manor, several tenant farms, and some privileged enterprises such as a mill. Modern Landed property often consists of housing or industrial land, generating income in the form of rents or fees for services provided by facilities on the land, such as port facilities.
Incentive	In economics and sociology, an Incentive is any factor (financial or non-financial) that enables or motivates a particular course of action, the study of Incentive structures is central to the study of all economic activity (both in terms of individual decision-making and in terms of co-operation and competition within a larger institutional structure).
Leasing	leasing is a process by which a firm can obtain the use of a certain fixed assets for which it must pay a series of contractual, periodic, tax deductible payments. The lessee is the receiver of the services or the assets under the lease contract and the lessor is the owner of the assets. The relationship between the tenant and the landlord is called a tenancy, and can be for a fixed or an indefinite period of time (called the term of the lease).
Production	Production refers to the economic process of converting of inputs into outputs and is a field of study in microeconomics. Production uses resources to create a good or service that is suitable for exchange. This can include manufacturing, storing, shipping, and packaging.
Production function	In economics, a Production function is a function that specifies the output of a firm, an industry) compares the practice of the existing entities converting inputs X into output y to determine the most efficient practice Production function of the existing entities, whether the most efficient feasible practice production or the most efficient actual practice production. In either case, the maximum output of a technologically-determined production process is a mathematical function of input factors of production.
Marginal product	In economics, the Marginal product or marginal physical product is the extra output produced by one more unit of an input . Assuming that no other inputs to production change, the Marginal product of a given input (X) can be expressed as: Marginal product = $\Delta Y/\Delta X$ = (the change of Y)/(the change of X).

In neoclassical economics, this is the mathematical derivative of the production function....

Reduced cost

In linear programming, Reduced cost, is the amount by which an objective function would have to improve (so increase for maximization problem, decrease for minimization problem) before it would be possible for a corresponding variable to assume a positive value in the optimal solution. It is cost for increasing a variable by a small amount, i.e., the first derivative from a certain point on the polyhedron that constraints the problem. When the point is a vertex in the polyhedron, the variable with the most extreme cost, negatively for minimisation and positively maximisation, is sometimes referred to as the steepest edge.

Economic growth

Economic growth is an increase in activity in an economy. It is often measured as the rate of change of gross domestic product (GDP). Economic growth refers only to the quantity of goods and services produced; it says nothing about the way in which they are produced.

Maximization

Maximization is an economics theory, that refers to individuals or societies gaining the maximum amount out of the resources they have available to them. The theory proposed by most economists is that Maximization refers to the Maximization of profit.

As some economists have begun to find out, this theory does not hold true for all people and cultures. The profit motive is not universal, and the profit motive does not seem to be applicable in all cases. Furthermore, Maximization does not ensure optimization; i.e. the maximum level of resource use is not necessarily the optimal level.

Yield

Yield is the compound rate of return that includes the effect of reinvesting interest or dividends.

To the right is an example of a stock investment of one share purchased at the beginning of the year for $100.

· The quarterly dividend is reinvested at the quarter-end stock price.
· The number of shares purchased each quarter = ($ Dividend)/($ Stock Price).
· The final investment value of $103.02 is a 3.02% Yield on the initial investment of $100. This is the compound Yield, and this return can be considered to be the return on the investment of $100.

To calculate the rate of return, the investor includes the reinvested dividends in the total investment. The investor received a total of $4.06 in dividends over the year, all of which were reinvested, so the investment amount increased by $4.06.

· Total Investment = Cost Basis = $100 + $4.06 = $104.06.
· Capital gain/loss = $103.02 - $104.06 = -$1.04 (a capital loss)
· ($4.06 dividends - $1.04 capital loss) / $104.06 total investment = 2.9% ROI

The disadvantage of this ROI calculation is that it does not take into account the fact that not all the money was invested during the entire year (the dividend reinvestments occurred throughout the year).

Risk aversion

Risk aversion is a concept in economics, finance, and psychology related to the behaviour of consumers and investors under uncertainty. Risk aversion is the reluctance of a person to accept a bargain with an uncertain payoff rather than another bargain with a more certain, but possibly lower, expected payoff. For example, a risk-averse investor might choose to put his or her money into a bank account with a low but guaranteed interest rate, rather than into a stock that is likely to have high returns, but also has a chance of becoming worthless.

Utility	In economics, Utility is a measure of the relative satisfaction from or desirability of, consumption of various goods and services. Given this measure, one may speak meaningfully of increasing or decreasing Utility, and thereby explain economic behavior in terms of attempts to increase one"s Utility. For illustrative purposes, changes in Utility are sometimes expressed in fictional units called utils (fictional in that there is no standard scale for them).
Principal-agent problem	In political science and economics, the Principal-agent problem or agency dilemma treats the difficulties that arise under conditions of incomplete and asymmetric information when a principal hires an agent, such as the problem that the two may not have the same interests, while the principal is, presumably, hiring the agent to pursue the interests of the former.
	Various mechanisms may be used to try to align the interests of the agent in solidarity with those of the principal, such as piece rates/commissions, profit sharing, efficiency wages, performance measurement (including financial statements), the agent posting a bond, or fear of firing. The Principal-agent problem is found in most employer/employee relationships, for example, when stockholders hire top executives of corporations.
Wage	Several countries have enacted a statutory minimum Wage rate that sets a price floor for certain kinds of labor. Wage derives from words which suggest "making a promise," often in monetary form. Specifically from the Old French word wagier or gagier meaning to pledge or promise, from which the money placed in a bet also derives.
Sharing	Sharing is the joint use of a resource or space. In its narrow sense, it refers to joint or alternating use of an inherently finite good, such as a common pasture or a shared residence. It is also the process of dividing and distributing.
Liability	In financial accounting, a Liability is defined as an obligation of an entity arising from past transactions or events, the settlement of which may result in the transfer or use of assets, provision of services or other yielding of economic benefits in the future.
	· All type of borrowing from persons or banks for improving a business or person income which is payable during short or long time. · They embody a duty or responsibility to others that entails settlement by future transfer or use of assets, provision of services or other yielding of economic benefits, at a specified or determinable date, on occurrence of a specified event, or on demand; · The duty or responsibility obligates the entity leaving it little or no discretion to avoid it; and, · The transaction or event obligating the entity has already occurred. Liabilities in financial accounting need not be legally enforceable; but can be based on equitable obligations or constructive obligations. An equitable obligation is a duty based on ethical or moral considerations.
Limited liability	Limited liability is a concept whereby a person"s financial liability is limited to a fixed sum, most commonly the value of a person"s investment in a company or partnership with Limited liability. In other words, if a company with Limited liability is sued, then the plaintiffs are suing the company, not its owners or investors. A shareholder in a limited company is not personally liable for any of the debts of the company, other than for the value of his investment in that company.

Screening	Screening in economics refers to a strategy of combating adverse selection, one of the potential decision-making complications in cases of asymmetric information. The concept of Screening is first developed by Michael Spence (1973), and should be distinguished from signalling, which implies that the informed agent moves first. For purposes of Screening, asymmetric information cases assume two economic agents--which we call, for example, Abel and Cain--where Abel knows more about himself than Cain knows about Abel.
Eviction	Eviction is the removal of a tenant from rental property by the landlord. Depending on the laws of the jurisdiction, Eviction may also be known as unlawful detainer, summary possession, summary dispossess, forcible detainer, ejectment, and repossession, among other terms. Nevertheless, the term Eviction is the most commonly used in communications between the landlord and tenant.
Information	Information as a concept has many meanings, from everyday usage to technical settings. The concept of Information is closely related to notions of constraint, communication, control, data, form, instruction, knowledge, meaning, mental stimulus, pattern, perception, and representation. The English word was apparently derived from the Latin accusative form of the nominative (informatio): this noun is in its turn derived from the verb "informare" (to inform) in the sense of "to give form to the mind", "to discipline", "instruct", "teach": "Men so wise should go and inform their kings." (1330) Inform itself comes from the Latin verb informare, to give form to, to form an idea of.
OPEC	The OPEC is a cartel of twelve countries made up of Algeria, Angola, Ecuador, Iran, Iraq, Kuwait, Libya, Nigeria, Qatar, Saudi Arabia, the United Arab Emirates, and Venezuela. OPEC has maintained its headquarters in Vienna since 1965, and hosts regular meetings among the oil ministers of its Member Countries. Indonesia withdrew its membership in OPEC in 2008 after it became a net importer of oil, but stated it would likely return if it became a net exporter in the world again.
Operation Barga	Operation Barga was a Land Reforms movement throughout rural West Bengal for recording the names of sharecroppers (bargadars) while avoiding the time-consuming method of recording through the settlement machinery. It bestowed on the bargadars, the legal protection against eviction by the landlords, and entitled them to the due share of the produce. Operation Barga was launched in 1978 and concluded by the mid 80"s.
Efficient markets hypothesis	In finance, the efficient-market hypothesis asserts that financial markets are "informationally efficient", stocks, bonds, or property) already reflect all known information, and instantly change to reflect new information. Therefore, according to theory, it is impossible to consistently outperform the market by using any information that the market already knows, except through luck. Information or news in the Efficient markets hypothesis is defined as anything that may affect prices that is unknowable in the present and thus appears randomly in the future.
Property right	A property right is the exclusive authority to determine how a resource is used, whether that resource is owned by government or by individuals. All economic goods have a property rights attribute. This attribute has three broad components · The right to use the good · The right to earn income from the good · The right to transfer the good to others

The concept of property rights as used by economists and legal scholars are related but distinct. The distinction is largely seen in the economists'' focus on the ability of an individual or collective to control the use of the good.

Total-factor productivity	In economics, total-factor productivity (TFP) is a variable which accounts for effects in total output not caused by inputs. For example, a year with unusually good weather will tend to have higher output, because bad weather hinders agricultural output. A variable like weather does not directly relate to unit inputs, so weather is considered a total-factor productivity variable.
Factor	A factor or limiting resource is a factor that controls a process, such as organism growth or species population, size, or distribution. The availability of food, predation pressure, or availability of shelter are examples of factors that could be limiting for an organism. An example of a limiting factor is sunlight, which is crucial in rainforests.
Insurance	Insurance, in law and economics, is a form of risk management primarily used to hedge against the risk of a contingent loss. Insurance is defined as the equitable transfer of the risk of a loss, from one entity to another, in exchange for a premium, and can be thought of as a guaranteed and known small loss to prevent a large, possibly devastating loss. An insurer is a company selling the Insurance; an insured or policyholder is the person or entity buying the Insurance.
Lump-sum Tax	A Lump-sum tax is a tax that is a fixed amount no matter what the change in circumstance of the taxed entity. (A lump-sum subsidy or lump-sum redistribution is defined similarly). It is a regressive tax, such that the lower income is, the higher percentage of income applicable to the tax.
Wage rate	Several countries have enacted a statutory minimum wage rate that sets a price floor for certain kinds of labor. Wage derives from words which suggest "making a promise," often in monetary form. Specifically from the Old French word wagier or gagier meaning to pledge or promise, from which the money placed in a bet also derives.
Returns to scale	In economics, Returns to scale and economies of scale are related terms that describe what happens as the scale of production increases. They are different terms and should not be used interchangeably. .
Land reform	Land reforms (also agrarian reform, though that can have a broader meaning) is an often-controversial alteration in the societal arrangements whereby government administers possession and use of land. Land reform may consist of a government-initiated or government-backed real estate property redistribution, generally of agricultural land, or be part of an even more revolutionary program that may include forcible removal of an existing government that is seen to oppose such reforms. Throughout history, popular discontent with land-related institutions has been one of the most common factors in provoking revolutionary movements and other social upheavals.
Redistribution	In economics, redistribution is the transfer of income, wealth or property from some individuals to others. Income redistribution evens the amount of income that individuals are permitted to earn, in order to correct the ineffectiveness of a market economy to remunerate based on the amount of labor expended by an individual. The objective of moderate income redistribution is to avoid the unjust equalization of incomes on one side and unjust extremes of concentration on the other sides.

Moral hazard	Moral hazard is the fact that a party insulated from risk may behave differently from the way it would behave if it would be fully exposed to the risk. In insurance, Moral hazard that occurs without conscious or malicious action is called morale hazard.
	Moral hazard is a special case of information asymmetry, a situation in which one party in a transaction has more information than another.
Participation	In finance, a Bond+Option is a capital guarantee product that provides an investor with a fixed, predetermined Participation to an option. Buying the zero-coupon bond ensures the guarantee of the capital, and the remaining proceeds are used to buy an option.
	As an example, we can consider a bond+call on 5 years, with Nokia as an underlying. Say it is a USD currency option, and that 5 year rates are 4.7%. That gives you a zero-coupon bond price of $$ZCB(USD, 5y, 4.7\%) = e^{-5*0.047} \approx 0.7906$$
Indifference curve	In microeconomic theory, an Indifference curve is a graph showing different bundles of goods, each measured as to quantity, between which a consumer is indifferent. That is, at each point on the curve, the consumer has no preference for one bundle over another. In other words, they are all equally preferred.
Scatter plot	A scatter plot is a type of mathematical diagram using Cartesian coordinates to display values for two variables for a set of data.
	The data is displayed as a collection of points, each having the value of one variable determining the position on the horizontal axis and the value of the other variable determining the position on the vertical axis. A scatter plot is also called a scatter chart, scatter diagram and scatter graph.
Mean	In statistics, mean has two related meanings:
	· the arithmetic mean .
	· the expected value of a random variable, which is also called the population mean.
	It is sometimes stated that the "mean" means average. This is incorrect if "mean" is taken in the specific sense of "arithmetic mean" as there are different types of averages: the mean, median, and mode.

Principal-agent problem	In political science and economics, the Principal-agent problem or agency dilemma treats the difficulties that arise under conditions of incomplete and asymmetric information when a principal hires an agent, such as the problem that the two may not have the same interests, while the principal is, presumably, hiring the agent to pursue the interests of the former. Various mechanisms may be used to try to align the interests of the agent in solidarity with those of the principal, such as piece rates/commissions, profit sharing, efficiency wages, performance measurement (including financial statements), the agent posting a bond, or fear of firing. The Principal-agent problem is found in most employer/employee relationships, for example, when stockholders hire top executives of corporations.
Labor supply	In mainstream economic theories, the Labor supply is the number of total hours that workers wish to work at a given real wage rate. Realistically, the Labor supply is a function of various factors within an economy. For instance, overpopulation increases the number of available workers driving down wages and can result in high unemployment.
Demand	In economics, demand is the desire to own anything and the ability to pay for it. . The term demand signifies the ability or the willingness to buy a particular commodity at a given point of time.
Supply and demand	Supply and demand is an economic model based on price, utility and quantity in a market. It concludes that in a competitive market, price will function to equalize the quantity demanded by consumers, and the quantity supplied by producers, resulting in an economic equilibrium of price and quantity. The demand schedule, depicted graphically as the demand curve, represents the amount of goods that buyers are willing and able to purchase at various prices, assuming all other non-price factors remain the same.
Dot-com bubble	The "Dot-com bubble" (or) was a speculative bubble covering roughly 1998-2001 (with a climax on March 10, 2000 with the NASDAQ peaking at 5132.52) during which stock markets in Western nations saw their equity value rise rapidly from growth in the more recent Internet sector and related fields. While the latter part was a boom and bust cycle, the Internet boom sometimes is meant to refer to the steady commercial growth of the Internet with the advent of the world wide web as exemplified by the first release of the Mosaic web browser in 1993 and continuing through the 1990s. The period was marked by the founding (and, in many cases, spectacular failure) of a group of new Internet-based companies commonly referred to as dot-coms.
Unemployment	Unemployment occurs when a person is available to work and seeking work but currently without work. The prevalence of Unemployment is usually measured using the Unemployment rate, which is defined as the percentage of those in the labor force who are unemployed. The Unemployment rate is also used in economic studies and economic indices such as the United States" Conference Board"s Index of Leading Indicators as a measure of the state of the macroeconomics.
Wage	Several countries have enacted a statutory minimum Wage rate that sets a price floor for certain kinds of labor. Wage derives from words which suggest "making a promise," often in monetary form. Specifically from the Old French word wagier or gagier meaning to pledge or promise, from which the money placed in a bet also derives.
Mean	In statistics, mean has two related meanings: · the arithmetic mean . · the expected value of a random variable, which is also called the population mean.

It is sometimes stated that the "mean" means average. This is incorrect if "mean" is taken in the specific sense of "arithmetic mean" as there are different types of averages: the mean, median, and mode.

Nutrition	Nutrition is the provision, to cells and organisms, of the materials necessary (in the form of food) to support life. Many common health problems can be prevented or alleviated with a healthy diet.
	Nutriton is a process of intake of nutrients (like carbohydrates, fats, proteins, Vitamins, minerals and water) by the organism as well as the utilisation of these nutrients by the organism.
Demand curve	In economics, the Demand curve can be defined as the graph depicting the relationship between the price of a certain commodity, and the amount of it that consumers are willing and able to purchase at that given price. It is a graphic representation of a demand schedule. The Demand curve for all consumers together follows from the Demand curve of every individual consumer: the individual demands at each price are added together.
Market equilibrium	In economics, economic equilibrium is simply a state of the world where economic forces are balanced and in the absence of external influences the (equilibrium) values of economic variables will not change. It is the point at which quantity demanded and quantity supplied are equal. Market equilibrium, for example, refers to a condition where a market price is established through competition such that the amount of goods or services sought by buyers is equal to the amount of goods or services produced by sellers.
Asset	In business and accounting, Assets are economic resources owned by business or company. Anything tangible or intangible that one possesses, usually considered as applicable to the payment of one"s debts is considered an Asset. Simplistically stated, Assets are things of value that can be readily converted into cash (although cash itself is also considered an Asset).
Self-employment	Self-employment is where a person works for themselves rather than someone else or a company that they do not own. To be self-employed, an individual is normally highly skilled in a trade or has a niche product or service for their local community. With the creation of the Internet the ability for an individual to become self-employed has increased dramatically.
Land reform	Land reforms (also agrarian reform, though that can have a broader meaning) is an often-controversial alteration in the societal arrangements whereby government administers possession and use of land. Land reform may consist of a government-initiated or government-backed real estate property redistribution, generally of agricultural land, or be part of an even more revolutionary program that may include forcible removal of an existing government that is seen to oppose such reforms.
	Throughout history, popular discontent with land-related institutions has been one of the most common factors in provoking revolutionary movements and other social upheavals.
Change	changes can refer to: · A jazz term for chord progression

101

· changes (band), an American folk band

· The changes (band), an American rock band

· changes (The Monkees album), The Monkees" ninth studio album

· changes, Christopher Wiliams" second studio album

· changes, an album by R. Carlos Nakai

· changes (Taylor Horn album), Taylor Horn"s third studio album

· changesbowie, a David Bowie compilation album

· changes (Kelly Osbourne album), Kelly Osbourne"s second studio album

· changes (Vanilla Sky album), Vanilla Sky"s third album

· changes (Jarrett album), by Keith Jarrett, Jack DeJohnette and Gary Peacock

· changes (Billy "Crash" Craddock album)

· changes (Lisa Miskovsky album)

· changes (Tanya Tucker album)

· changes, an album by Johnny Rivers

· "changes" (David Bowie song), a song by David Bowie on his 1971 album Hunky Dory

· "changes" (2Pac song), a song by Tupac Shakur on his Greatest Hits album

· "changes" (Black Sabbath song), a ballad by Black Sabbath, remade as a duet by Kelly and Ozzy Osbourne

· "changes" (Will Young song), a song by Will Young on his fourth studio album, Let It Go

· "changes" (Gareth Gates song), a song by Gareth Gates, from the album Pictures of the Other Side

· "changes" (Imagination song), a song by Imagination, from the album In the Heat of the Night

· "changes", a song by Yes on the album 90125

· "changes", a song by "Buddy" Miles ' Jimi Hendrix on the album Band of Gypsys

· "changes", a song by Jane"s Addiction

· "changes", a song by Phil Ochs

· "changes", a song by Godsmack on the album Faceless

· "changes", a song by The Zombies on the album Odessey and Oracle

· "changes", a song by 3 Doors Down on the album Away from the Sun

· "changes", a song by Sugar on the album Copper Blue

· "changes", a song by Chris Lake

· "changes", a song by Moby Grape on their album Moby Grape

· "changes", a song by Santana on their album Zebop!

· The changes (TV series), produced by the BBC in 1975. Also the changes Trilogy of novels on which the series was based, written by Peter Dickinson .

Time horizon

A Time horizon, also known as a planning horizon, is a fixed point of time in the future at which point certain processes will be evaluated or assumed to end. It is necessary in an accounting, finance or risk management regime to assign such a fixed horizon time so that alternatives can be evaluated for performance over the same period of time. A Time horizon is a physical impossibility in the real world.

Anecdotal value	In economics, Anecdotal value refers to the primarily social and political value of an anecdote or anecdotal evidence in promoting understanding of a social, cultural, in the last several decades the evaluation of anecdotes has received sustained academic scrutiny from economists and scholars such as S.G. Checkland (on David Ricardo), Steven Novella, Hollis Robbins, R. Charleton, Kwamena Kwansah-Aidoo, and others; these academics seek to quantify the value inherent in the deployment of anecdotes. More recently, economists studying choice models have begun assessing Anecdotal value in the context of framing; Kahneman and Tversky suggest that choice models may be contingent on stories or anecdotes that frame or influence choice.
Rural	Rural areas (referred to as "the countryside") are large and isolated areas of a country, often with low population density. About 91 percent of the Rural population now earn salaried incomes, often in urban areas. The 10 percent who still produce resources generate 20 percent of the world"s coal, copper, and oil; 10 percent of its wheat, 20 percent of its meat, and 50 percent of its corn.
Capital costs	Capital costs are costs incurred on the purchase of land, buildings, construction and equipment to be used in the production of goods or the rendering of services. In other words, the total cost needed to bring a project to a commercially operable status. However, Capital costs are not limited to the initial construction of a factory or other business.
Production	Production refers to the economic process of converting of inputs into outputs and is a field of study in microeconomics. Production uses resources to create a good or service that is suitable for exchange. This can include manufacturing, storing, shipping, and packaging.
Cost of Capital	In business and finance, the Cost of capital is the cost of obtaining funds for, or, conversely, the required return necessary to meet its cost of financing a capital budgeting project. Said another way, it is "the minimum return that a company should make on its own investments, to earn the cash flow out of which investors can be paid their return." Cost of capital encompasses the two fundamental sources of financing: the cost of debt (including bonds and loans) and the cost of equity. Capital (money) used for funding a business should earn returns for the capital providers who risk their capital.
Seasonality	In statistics, many time series exhibit cyclic variation known as Seasonality, periodic variation or periodic fluctuations. This variation can be either regular or semiregular. For example, retail sales tend to peak for the Christmas season and then decline after the holidays.
Tenancy	Leasing is a process by which a firm can obtain the use of a certain fixed assets for which it must pay a series of contractual, periodic, tax deductible payments. The lessee is the receiver of the services or the assets under the lease contract and the lessor is the owner of the assets. The relationship between the tenant and the landlord is called a tenancy, and can be for a fixed or an indefinite period of time (called the term of the lease).
Marginal product	In economics, the Marginal product or marginal physical product is the extra output produced by one more unit of an input . Assuming that no other inputs to production change, the Marginal product of a given input (X) can be expressed as: Marginal product = $\Delta Y/\Delta X$ = (the change of Y)/(the change of X).

In neoclassical economics, this is the mathematical derivative of the production function....

Risk aversion

Risk aversion is a concept in economics, finance, and psychology related to the behaviour of consumers and investors under uncertainty. Risk aversion is the reluctance of a person to accept a bargain with an uncertain payoff rather than another bargain with a more certain, but possibly lower, expected payoff. For example, a risk-averse investor might choose to put his or her money into a bank account with a low but guaranteed interest rate, rather than into a stock that is likely to have high returns, but also has a chance of becoming worthless.

Utility

In economics, Utility is a measure of the relative satisfaction from or desirability of, consumption of various goods and services. Given this measure, one may speak meaningfully of increasing or decreasing Utility, and thereby explain economic behavior in terms of attempts to increase one"s Utility. For illustrative purposes, changes in Utility are sometimes expressed in fictional units called utils (fictional in that there is no standard scale for them).

Marginal Utility

In economics, the Marginal utility of a good or of a service is the utility of the specific use to which an agent would put a given increase in that good or service, Marginal utility is the utility of the marginal use -- which, on the assumption of economic rationality, would be the least urgent use of the good or service, from the best feasible combination of actions in which its use is included. Under the mainstream assumptions, the Marginal utility of a good or service is the posited quantified change in utility obtained by increasing or by decreasing use of that good or service.

Smoothing

In statistics and image processing, Smoothing a data set is to create an approximating function that attempts to capture important patterns in the data, while leaving out noise or other fine-scale structures/rapid phenomena. Many different algorithms are used in Smoothing. One of the most common algorithms is the "moving average", often used to try to capture important trends in repeated statistical surveys.

Information

Information as a concept has many meanings, from everyday usage to technical settings. The concept of Information is closely related to notions of constraint, communication, control, data, form, instruction, knowledge, meaning, mental stimulus, pattern, perception, and representation.

The English word was apparently derived from the Latin accusative form of the nominative (informatio): this noun is in its turn derived from the verb "informare" (to inform) in the sense of "to give form to the mind", "to discipline", "instruct", "teach": "Men so wise should go and inform their kings." (1330) Inform itself comes from the Latin verb informare, to give form to, to form an idea of.

Bond market	The Bond market is a financial market where participants buy and sell debt securities, usually in the form of bonds. As of 2008, the size of the international Bond market is an estimated $67.0 trillion , of which the size of the outstanding U.S. Bond market debt was $33.5 trillion. Nearly all of the $923 billion average daily trading volume (as of early 2007) in the U.S. Bond market takes place between broker-dealers and large institutions in a decentralized, over-the-counter (OTC) market.
Insurance	Insurance, in law and economics, is a form of risk management primarily used to hedge against the risk of a contingent loss. Insurance is defined as the equitable transfer of the risk of a loss, from one entity to another, in exchange for a premium, and can be thought of as a guaranteed and known small loss to prevent a large, possibly devastating loss. An insurer is a company selling the Insurance; an insured or policyholder is the person or entity buying the Insurance.
Loan	A Loan is a type of debt. Like all debt instruments, a Loan entails the redistribution of financial assets over time, between the lender and the borrower. In a Loan, the borrower initially receives or borrows an amount of money, called the principal, from the lender, and is obligated to pay back or repay an equal amount of money to the lender at a later time.
Crop Insurance	Crop insurance is purchased by agricultural producers, including farmers, ranchers, and others to protect themselves against either the loss of their crops due to natural disasters, such as hail, drought, and floods or the loss of revenue due to declines in the prices of agricultural commodities. The two general categories of Crop insurance are called crop-yield insurance and crop-revenue insurance.
Seasonality	In statistics, many time series exhibit cyclic variation known as Seasonality, periodic variation or periodic fluctuations. This variation can be either regular or semiregular. For example, retail sales tend to peak for the Christmas season and then decline after the holidays.
Demand	In economics, demand is the desire to own anything and the ability to pay for it. . The term demand signifies the ability or the willingness to buy a particular commodity at a given point of time.
Working Capital	Working capital, also known as net Working capital or NWC, is a financial metric which represents operating liquidity available to a business. Along with fixed assets such as plant and equipment, Working capital is considered a part of operating capital. It is calculated as current assets minus current liabilities.
Monopoly	In economics, a Monopoly exists when a specific individual or an enterprise has sufficient control over a particular product or service to determine significantly the terms on which other individuals shall have access to it. Monopolies are thus characterized by a lack of economic competition for the good or service that they provide and a lack of viable substitute goods. The verb "monopolize" refers to the process by which a firm gains persistently greater market share than what is expected under perfect competition.
Rural	Rural areas (referred to as "the countryside") are large and isolated areas of a country, often with low population density. About 91 percent of the Rural population now earn salaried incomes, often in urban areas. The 10 percent who still produce resources generate 20 percent of the world"s coal, copper, and oil; 10 percent of its wheat, 20 percent of its meat, and 50 percent of its corn.

Credit risk	Credit risk is the risk of loss due to a debtor"s non-payment of a loan or other line of credit (either the principal or interest (coupon) or both).
	Most lenders employ their own models (credit scorecards) to rank potential and existing customers according to risk, and then apply appropriate strategies. With products such as unsecured personal loans or mortgages, lenders charge a higher price for higher risk customers and vice versa.
Liability	In financial accounting, a Liability is defined as an obligation of an entity arising from past transactions or events, the settlement of which may result in the transfer or use of assets, provision of services or other yielding of economic benefits in the future.
	· All type of borrowing from persons or banks for improving a business or person income which is payable during short or long time. · They embody a duty or responsibility to others that entails settlement by future transfer or use of assets, provision of services or other yielding of economic benefits, at a specified or determinable date, on occurrence of a specified event, or on demand; · The duty or responsibility obligates the entity leaving it little or no discretion to avoid it; and, · The transaction or event obligating the entity has already occurred. Liabilities in financial accounting need not be legally enforceable; but can be based on equitable obligations or constructive obligations. An equitable obligation is a duty based on ethical or moral considerations.
Limited liability	Limited liability is a concept whereby a person"s financial liability is limited to a fixed sum, most commonly the value of a person"s investment in a company or partnership with Limited liability. In other words, if a company with Limited liability is sued, then the plaintiffs are suing the company, not its owners or investors. A shareholder in a limited company is not personally liable for any of the debts of the company, other than for the value of his investment in that company.
Rate of return	Yield is the compound Rate of return that includes the effect of reinvesting interest or dividends.
	To the right is an example of a stock investment of one share purchased at the beginning of the year for $100.
	· The quarterly dividend is reinvested at the quarter-end stock price. · The number of shares purchased each quarter = ($ Dividend)/($ Stock Price). · The final investment value of $103.02 is a 3.02% Yield on the initial investment of $100. This is the compound yield, and this return can be considered to be the return on the investment of $100. To calculate the Rate of return, the investor includes the reinvested dividends in the total investment. The investor received a total of $4.06 in dividends over the year, all of which were reinvested, so the investment amount increased by $4.06.
	· Total Investment = Cost Basis = $100 + $4.06 = $104.06. · Capital gain/loss = $103.02 - $104.06 = -$1.04 (a capital loss) · ($4.06 dividends - $1.04 capital loss) / $104.06 total investment = 2.9% ROI The disadvantage of this ROI calculation is that it does not take into account the fact that not all the money was invested during the entire year (the dividend reinvestments occurred throughout the year).

Dot-com bubble	The "Dot-com bubble" (or) was a speculative bubble covering roughly 1998-2001 (with a climax on March 10, 2000 with the NASDAQ peaking at 5132.52) during which stock markets in Western nations saw their equity value rise rapidly from growth in the more recent Internet sector and related fields. While the latter part was a boom and bust cycle, the Internet boom sometimes is meant to refer to the steady commercial growth of the Internet with the advent of the world wide web as exemplified by the first release of the Mosaic web browser in 1993 and continuing through the 1990s.
	The period was marked by the founding (and, in many cases, spectacular failure) of a group of new Internet-based companies commonly referred to as dot-coms.
Credit union	A Credit union is a cooperative financial institution that is owned and controlled by its members, and operated for the purpose of promoting thrift, providing credit at reasonable rates, and providing other financial services to its members. Many Credit unions exist to further community development or sustainable international development on a local level. Worldwide, Credit union systems vary significantly in terms of total system assets and average institution asset size since Credit unions exist in a wide range of sizes, ranging from volunteer operations with a handful of members to institutions with several billion dollars in assets and hundreds of thousands of members.
Marketing	Marketing is an integrated communications-based process through which individuals and communities are informed or persuaded that existing and newly-identified needs and wants may be satisfied by the products and services of others.
Agent	Agent most commonly refers to:

Agent most commonly refers to:

· an entity that is capable of action, or "agency"
· one who acts for, or in the place of another, (the principal), by authority from him
· a title or honorific, such as "Agent Smith"

· Agent provocateur, person employed by the police or other entity to act undercover to entice or provoke another person to commit an illegal act
· Double Agent, counterintelligence term for someone who pretends to spy on a target organization on behalf of a controlling organization, but in fact is loyal to the target organization

· Triple Agent, pretends to be a double Agent for the target organization, but in fact is working for the controlling organization all along
· Special Agent, title for a detective or investigator for a state, county, municipal, federal or tribal government
· Secret Agent, spy involved in espionage

· Agent (law), in Commercial Law, is a person who is authorised to act on behalf of another (called the Principal) to create a legal relationship with a Third Party

· Election Agent, person legally responsible for the conduct of a candidate''s political campaign (UK)
· Free Agent, sports player whose contract with a team has expired
· Literary Agent, person who represents writers and their written works to publishers, theatrical producers and film producers
· Press Agent, professional publicist who acts on behalf of his or her client on all matters involving public relations
· Sports Agent, person who procures and negotiates employment and endorsement deals for a player
· Talent Agent or booking Agent, person who finds jobs for actors, musicians and models, etc., in various entertainment businesses
· Foreign Agent, person representing the interests of foreign powers, mandated by the Foreign Agents Registration Act to be identified to the American public
· Patent Agent or patent attorney, person who has the specialized qualifications necessary for representing clients in obtaining patents and acting in all matters and procedures relating to patent law and practice
· Real estate Agent or real estate broker, person who acts as an intermediary between sellers and buyers of real estate
· Travel Agent, person who works on behalf of a travel agency
· Tuition Agent, person who works on behalf of a tuition agency, specializing in introducing tutors to students requiring help in the academic area
· Yacht Agent or yacht broker, specialist who acts as a representative for the sale of a yacht or boat

· Agent , actor and decision maker in a model

· Homo economicus, concept in some economic theories of humans as rational and broadly self-interested actors
· Agent-Based Computational Economics, computational study of economic processes modeled as dynamic systems of interacting Agents
· Rational Agent, entity which has clear preferences, models uncertainty via expected values, and always chooses to perform the action that results in the optimal outcome for itself from among all feasible actions
· Representative Agent, refers to the typical decision-maker of a certain type

· A pharmacological Agent is a chemical substance with pharmacological or biological activity, i.e., a pharmaceutical drug

· Agent Orange, code name for an herbicide and defoliant
· Biological Agent, infectious disease or toxin that can be used in bioterrorism or biological warfare
· Chemical warfare, involves using the toxic properties of chemical substances as weapons to kill, injure, or incapacitate an enemy

· Blister Agent or vesicant, chemical compound that causes severe skin, eye and mucosal pain and irritation
· Blood Agent or cyanogen Agent, chemical compound carried by the blood for distribution throughout the body
· Incapacitating Agent, Agent that produces temporary physiological or mental effects, or both, which will render individuals incapable of concerted effort in the performance of their assigned duties
· Nerve Agent or nerve gases, class of phosphorus-containing organic chemicals (organophosphates) that disrupt the mechanism by which nerves transfer messages to organs
· Pulmonary Agent or choking Agent, chemical weapon Agent designed to impede a victim"s ability to breathe
· Riot control Agent, less-lethal lachrymatory Agents used for riot control

· Agent (grammar), the participant of a situation that carries out the action in this situation; also the name of the thematic role (also known as the thematic relation)
· Agent noun (or nomen Agentis), word that is derived from another word denoting an action, and that identifies an entity that does that action

· Agent architecture, blueprint for software Agents and intelligent control systems, depicting the arrangement of components
· Agent-based model, computational model for simulating the actions and interactions of autonomous individuals with a view to assessing their effects on the system as a whole
· Intelligent Agent, autonomous entity which observes and acts upon an environment and directs its activity towards achieving goals
· Software Agent, piece of software that acts for a user or other program in a relationship of agency

· Forté Agent, email and Usenet news client used on the Windows operating system
· User Agent, the client application used with a particular network protocol

· Agent 47, fictional character and protagonist in the Hitman video-game series.
· Agent 212, name of a humorous Belgian comic about a large police officer
· Agent , group of characters in the series
· Agent (video game), currently in development by Rockstar North for the Playstation 3
· The Agent (film), 1922 film featuring Oliver Hardy
· Secret Agent (1936 film), British film directed by Alfred Hitchcock
· Agent, version of The Mole (TV series) that aired in Poland on TVN
· The Agents, superhuman characters in Seven Samurai 20XX
· Agents (band), a Finnish schlager/rock"n"roll band .

Layering

layering is a means of plant propagation in which a portion of an aerial stem grow roots while still attached to the parent plant and then detaches as an independent plant. layering has evolved as a common means of vegetative propagation of numerous species in natural environments. layering is also utilized by horticulturists to propagate desirable plants.

Interest	In the Renaissance era, greater mobility of people facilitated an increase in commerce and the appearance of appropriate conditions for entrepreneurs to start new, lucrative businesses. Given that borrowed money was no longer strictly for consumption but for production as well, Interest was no longer viewed in the same manner. The School of Salamanca elaborated on various reasons that justified the charging of Interest: the person who received a loan benefited, and one could consider Interest as a premium paid for the risk taken by the loaning party.
Interest rate	An interest rate is the price a borrower pays for the use of money they do not own, for instance a small company might borrow from a bank to kick start their business, and the return a lender receives for deferring the use of funds, by lending it to the borrower. interest rates are normally expressed as a percentage rate over the period of one year.
	interest rates targets are also a vital tool of monetary policy and are used to control variables like investment, inflation, and unemployment.
Rationing	Rationing is the controlled distribution of resources and scarce goods or services. Rationing controls the size of the ration, one"s allotted portion of the resources being distributed on a particular day or at a particular time.
	In economics, it is often common to use the word "Rationing" to refer to one of the roles that prices play in markets, while Rationing (as the word is usually used) is called "non-price Rationing".
Rights	rights are entitlements or permissions, usually of a legal or moral nature. rights are of vital importance in the fields of law and ethics, especially theories of justice and deontology.
	There are numerous different theoretical distinctions in accordance with which rights may be classified.
Debt bondage	Debt bondage (or bonded labor) is an arrangement whereby a person is forced to pay off a loan with direct labor in place of currency, over an agreed or obscure period of time. When the debtor is then tricked or trapped into working for very little or no pay, or when the value of their work is significantly greater than the original sum of money borrowed, some consider the arrangement to be a form of unfree labour or debt slavery. It is similar to peonage, indenture or the truck system.
Time horizon	A Time horizon, also known as a planning horizon, is a fixed point of time in the future at which point certain processes will be evaluated or assumed to end. It is necessary in an accounting, finance or risk management regime to assign such a fixed horizon time so that alternatives can be evaluated for performance over the same period of time. A Time horizon is a physical impossibility in the real world.
Participation	In finance, a Bond+Option is a capital guarantee product that provides an investor with a fixed, predetermined Participation to an option. Buying the zero-coupon bond ensures the guarantee of the capital, and the remaining proceeds are used to buy an option.
	As an example, we can consider a bond+call on 5 years, with Nokia as an underlying. Say it is a USD currency option, and that 5 year rates are 4.7%. That gives you a zero-coupon bond price of $$ZCB(USD, 5y, 4.7\%) = e^{-5*0.047} \approx 0.7906$$

Observable	In physics, particularly in quantum physics, a system observable is a property of the system state that can be determined by some sequence of physical operations. For example, these operations might involve submitting the system to various electromagnetic fields and eventually reading a value off some gauge. In systems governed by classical mechanics, any experimentally observable value can be shown to be given by a real-valued function on the set of all possible system states.
Information	Information as a concept has many meanings, from everyday usage to technical settings. The concept of Information is closely related to notions of constraint, communication, control, data, form, instruction, knowledge, meaning, mental stimulus, pattern, perception, and representation.
	The English word was apparently derived from the Latin accusative form of the nominative (informatio): this noun is in its turn derived from the verb "informare" (to inform) in the sense of "to give form to the mind", "to discipline", "instruct", "teach": "Men so wise should go and inform their kings." (1330) Inform itself comes from the Latin verb informare, to give form to, to form an idea of.
Screening	Screening in economics refers to a strategy of combating adverse selection, one of the potential decision-making complications in cases of asymmetric information. The concept of Screening is first developed by Michael Spence (1973), and should be distinguished from signalling, which implies that the informed agent moves first.
	For purposes of Screening, asymmetric information cases assume two economic agents--which we call, for example, Abel and Cain--where Abel knows more about himself than Cain knows about Abel.
Cost	In business, retail, and accounting, a cost is the value of money that has been used up to produce something, and hence is not available for use anymore. In economics, a cost is an alternative that is given up as a result of a decision. In business, the cost may be one of acquisition, in which case the amount of money expended to acquire it is counted as cost.
Mortgage	A mortgage is the transfer of an interest in property (or the equivalent in law - a charge) to a lender as a security for a debt - usually a loan of money. While a mortgage in itself is not a debt, it is the lender"s security for a debt. It is a transfer of an interest in land (or the equivalent) from the owner to the mortgage lender, on the condition that this interest will be returned to the owner when the terms of the mortgage have been satisfied or performed.
Production	Production refers to the economic process of converting of inputs into outputs and is a field of study in microeconomics. Production uses resources to create a good or service that is suitable for exchange. This can include manufacturing, storing, shipping, and packaging.
Diminishing returns	In economics, Diminishing returns refers to how the marginal production of a factor of production, in contrast to the increase that would otherwise be normally expected, actually starts to progressively decrease the more of the factor are added. According to this relationship, in a production system with fixed and variable inputs (say factory size and labor), beyond some point, each additional unit of the variable input (IE man*hours) yields smaller and smaller increases in outputs, also reducing the mean productivity of each worker. Conversely, producing one more unit of output, costs more and more (due to the major amount of variable inputs being used,to little effect)
	This concept is also known as the law of diminishing marginal returns or the law of increasing relative cost.

Production function	In economics, a Production function is a function that specifies the output of a firm, an industry) compares the practice of the existing entities converting inputs X into output y to determine the most efficient practice Production function of the existing entities, whether the most efficient feasible practice production or the most efficient actual practice production. In either case, the maximum output of a technologically-determined production process is a mathematical function of input factors of production.
Tax profit	Tax profit or taxable profit is used to distinguish between accounting profit or earnings (the number that is generally referred to in financial results for public companies and quoted in the press). Taxable profit is the number that is used to calculate profit tax.
	For a number of reasons, taxable profit may differ from reported earnings, and may be higher or lower.
Incentive	In economics and sociology, an Incentive is any factor (financial or non-financial) that enables or motivates a particular course of action, the study of Incentive structures is central to the study of all economic activity (both in terms of individual decision-making and in terms of co-operation and competition within a larger institutional structure).

Consumption smoothing	Consumption smoothing is an economic concept which refers to balancing out spending and saving to attain and maintain the highest possible living standard over the course of one"s life. This idea is notable because of its difference in approach to common knowledge about preparing for retirement, in which individuals are encouraged to save a particular % of their income throughout their life. Some believe that this approach is flawed and typically leads to one of two outcomes: over-saving or over-spending.
Insurance	Insurance, in law and economics, is a form of risk management primarily used to hedge against the risk of a contingent loss. Insurance is defined as the equitable transfer of the risk of a loss, from one entity to another, in exchange for a premium, and can be thought of as a guaranteed and known small loss to prevent a large, possibly devastating loss. An insurer is a company selling the Insurance; an insured or policyholder is the person or entity buying the Insurance.
Crop Insurance	Crop insurance is purchased by agricultural producers, including farmers, ranchers, and others to protect themselves against either the loss of their crops due to natural disasters, such as hail, drought, and floods or the loss of revenue due to declines in the prices of agricultural commodities. The two general categories of Crop insurance are called crop-yield insurance and crop-revenue insurance.
Shock	In economics a shock is an unexpected or unpredictable event that affects an economy, either positively or negatively. Technically, it refers to an unpredictable change in exogenous factors -- that is, factors unexplained by economics -- which may have an impact on endogenous economic variables.
	The response of economic variables, like output and employment, at the time of the shock and at subsequent times, is called an impulse response function.
Trade	Trade is the voluntary exchange of goods, services, or both. Trade is also called commerce or transaction. A mechanism that allows Trade is called a market.
Alternative hypothesis	In statistical hypothesis testing, the Alternative hypothesis (or maintained hypothesis or research hypothesis) and the null hypothesis are the two rival hypotheses which are compared by a statistical hypothesis test. An example might be where water quality in a stream has been observed over many years and a test is made of the null hypothesis that there is no change in quality between the first and second halves of the data against the Alternative hypothesis that the quality is poorer in the second half of the record.
	The concept of an Alternative hypothesis in testing was devised by Jerzy Neyman and Egon Pearson, and it is used in the Neyman-Pearson lemma.
Hypothesis testing	A statistical hypothesis test is a method of making statistical decisions using experimental data. In statistics, a result is called statistically significant if it is unlikely to have occurred by chance. The phrase "test of significance" was coined by Ronald Fisher: "Critical tests of this kind may be called tests of significance, and when such tests are available we may discover whether a second sample is or is not significantly different from the first."
	hypothesis testing is sometimes called confirmatory data analysis, in contrast to exploratory data analysis.
Information	Information as a concept has many meanings, from everyday usage to technical settings. The concept of Information is closely related to notions of constraint, communication, control, data, form, instruction, knowledge, meaning, mental stimulus, pattern, perception, and representation.

The English word was apparently derived from the Latin accusative form of the nominative (informatio): this noun is in its turn derived from the verb "informare" (to inform) in the sense of "to give form to the mind", "to discipline", "instruct", "teach": "Men so wise should go and inform their kings." (1330) Inform itself comes from the Latin verb informare, to give form to, to form an idea of.

Incentive	In economics and sociology, an Incentive is any factor (financial or non-financial) that enables or motivates a particular course of action, the study of Incentive structures is central to the study of all economic activity (both in terms of individual decision-making and in terms of co-operation and competition within a larger institutional structure).
Moral hazard	Moral hazard is the fact that a party insulated from risk may behave differently from the way it would behave if it would be fully exposed to the risk. In insurance, Moral hazard that occurs without conscious or malicious action is called morale hazard.
	Moral hazard is a special case of information asymmetry, a situation in which one party in a transaction has more information than another.
Utility	In economics, Utility is a measure of the relative satisfaction from or desirability of, consumption of various goods and services. Given this measure, one may speak meaningfully of increasing or decreasing Utility, and thereby explain economic behavior in terms of attempts to increase one"s Utility. For illustrative purposes, changes in Utility are sometimes expressed in fictional units called utils (fictional in that there is no standard scale for them).
Coordination game	In game theory, Coordination games are a class of games with multiple pure strategy Nash equilibria in which players choose the same or corresponding strategies. Coordination games are a formalization of the idea of a coordination problem, which is widespread in the social sciences, including economics, meaning situations in which all parties can realize mutual gains, but only by making mutually consistent decisions. A common application is the choice of technological standards.
Time horizon	A Time horizon, also known as a planning horizon, is a fixed point of time in the future at which point certain processes will be evaluated or assumed to end. It is necessary in an accounting, finance or risk management regime to assign such a fixed horizon time so that alternatives can be evaluated for performance over the same period of time. A Time horizon is a physical impossibility in the real world.

Nominative determinism	Nominative determinism refers to the theory that a person"s name is given an influential role in reflecting key attributes of his job, profession, but real examples are more highly prized, the more obscure the better.
Trade	Trade is the voluntary exchange of goods, services, or both. Trade is also called commerce or transaction. A mechanism that allows Trade is called a market.
Good	In macroeconomics and accounting, a good is contrasted with a service. In this sense, a good is defined as a physical (tangible) product, capable of being delivered to a purchaser and involves the transfer of ownership from seller to customer, say an apple, as opposed to an (intangible) service, say a haircut. A more general term that preserves the distinction between goods and services is "commodities," like a flashlight.
Price	price in economics and business is the result of an exchange and from that trade we assign a numerical monetary value to a good, service or asset. If Alice trades Bob 4 apples for an orange, the price of an orange is 4 apples. Inversely, the price of an apple is 1/4 oranges.
Production	Production refers to the economic process of converting of inputs into outputs and is a field of study in microeconomics. Production uses resources to create a good or service that is suitable for exchange. This can include manufacturing, storing, shipping, and packaging.
Purchasing power parity	The Purchasing power parity theory uses the long-term equilibrium exchange rate of two currencies to equalize their purchasing power. Developed by Gustav Cassel in 1918, it is based on the law of one price: the theory states that, in ideally efficient markets, identical goods should have only one price.
	This purchasing power SEM rate equalizes the purchasing power of different currencies in their home countries for a given basket of goods.
Demand	In economics, demand is the desire to own anything and the ability to pay for it. . The term demand signifies the ability or the willingness to buy a particular commodity at a given point of time.
Cost	In business, retail, and accounting, a cost is the value of money that has been used up to produce something, and hence is not available for use anymore. In economics, a cost is an alternative that is given up as a result of a decision. In business, the cost may be one of acquisition, in which case the amount of money expended to acquire it is counted as cost.
Heckscher-Ohlin model	The Heckscher-Ohlin model (H-O model) is a general equilibrium mathematical model of international trade, developed by Eli Heckscher and Bertil Ohlin at the Stockholm School of Economics. It builds on David Ricardo"s theory of comparative advantage by predicting patterns of commerce and production based on the factor endowments of a trading region. The model essentially says that countries will export products that utilize their abundant and cheap factor(s) of production and import products that utilize the countries" scarce factor(s).
Factor	A factor or limiting resource is a factor that controls a process, such as organism growth or species population, size, or distribution. The availability of food, predation pressure, or availability of shelter are examples of factors that could be limiting for an organism. An example of a limiting factor is sunlight, which is crucial in rainforests.

Factor endowment	In economics a country"s Factor endowment is commonly understood as the amount of land, labor, capital, and entrepreneurship that a country possesses and can exploit for manufacturing. Countries with a large endowment of resources tend to be more prosperous than those with a small endowment, all other things being equal. The development of sound institutions to access and equitably distribute these resources, however, is necessary in order for a country to obtain the greatest benefit from its Factor endowment.
Preference	Preference is a concept, used in the social sciences, particularly economics. It assumes a real or imagined "choice" between alternatives and the possibility of rank ordering of these alternatives, based on happiness, satisfaction, gratification, enjoyment, utility they provide. More generally, it can be seen as a source of motivation.
Economies of scale	Economies of scale, in microeconomics, are the cost advantages that a business obtains due to expansion. They are factors that cause a producer"s average cost per unit to fall as scale is increased. Economies of scale is a long run concept and refers to reductions in unit cost as the size of a facility, or scale, increases.
Competition	Co-operative Competition is based upon promoting mutual survival - "everyone wins". Adam Smith"s "invisible hand" is a process where individuals compete to improve their level of happiness but compete in a cooperative manner through peaceful exchange and without violating other people. Cooperative Competition focuses individuals/groups/organisms against the environment.
Intra-industry Trade	Intra-industry trade refers to the exchange of products belonging to the same industry. The term is usually applied to international trade, where the same kinds of goods and services are both imported and exported. Examples of this kind of trade include automobiles, foodstuffs and beverages, computers and minerals.

Production	Production refers to the economic process of converting of inputs into outputs and is a field of study in microeconomics. Production uses resources to create a good or service that is suitable for exchange. This can include manufacturing, storing, shipping, and packaging.
Trade	Trade is the voluntary exchange of goods, services, or both. Trade is also called commerce or transaction. A mechanism that allows Trade is called a market.
Distributive	In mathematics, and in particular in abstract algebra, distributivity is a property of binary operations that generalises the distributive law from elementary algebra. For example: $2 \times (1 + 3) = (2 \times 1) + (2 \times 3)$. In the left-hand side of the above equation, the 2 multiplies the sum of 1 and 3; on the right-hand side, it multiplies the 1 and the 3 individually, with the results added afterwards.
Gains Trade	Gains trade in economics refers to net benefits to agents from voluntary trading with each other. It is commonly described as resulting from: · specialization in production from division of labor, economies of scale, and relative availability of factor resources and in types of output by farms, businesses, location, and economies · a resulting increase in total output possibilities · trade through markets from sale of one type of output for other, more highly valued goods. Market incentives, such as reflected in prices of outputs and inputs, are theorized to attract factors of production, including labor, into activities according to comparative advantage, that is, for which they each have a low opportunity cost. The factor owners then use their increased income from such specialization to buy more-valued goods of which they would otherwise be high-cost producers, hence their gains from trade.
Heckscher-Ohlin model	The Heckscher-Ohlin model (H-O model) is a general equilibrium mathematical model of international trade, developed by Eli Heckscher and Bertil Ohlin at the Stockholm School of Economics. It builds on David Ricardo"s theory of comparative advantage by predicting patterns of commerce and production based on the factor endowments of a trading region. The model essentially says that countries will export products that utilize their abundant and cheap factor(s) of production and import products that utilize the countries" scarce factor(s).
Distribution	Distribution in economics refers to the way total output or income is distributed among individuals or among the factors of production (labor, land, and capital) (Samuelson and Nordhaus, 2001, p. 762). In general theory and the national income and product accounts, each unit of output corresponds to a unit of income. One use of national accounts is for classifying factor incomes and measuring their respective shares, as in National Income.
Capital accumulation	Most generally, the accumulation of capital refers simply to the gathering or amassment of objects of value; the increase in wealth; or the creation of wealth. Capital can be generally defined as assets invested with the expectation that their value will increase, usually because there is the expectation of profit, rent, interest, royalties, capital gain or some other kind of return. The definition of Capital accumulation is subject to controversy and ambiguities, because it could refer to a net addition to existing wealth, or to a redistribution of wealth.

Elawyering	The term Elawyering or e-lawyering is a neologism used to refer to the practice of law over the Internet, in a way more expansive than a mere legal related internet advertisement for a service, lawyer, Elawyering initiatives have been undertaken by the American Bar Association in order to reach a "latent market" of lower and middle class citizens in need of legal services. Lawyers practicing law online are also referred to as "virtual lawyers" and practice from virtual law offices.
Primary products	The primary sector of the economy involves changing natural resources into Primary products. Most products from this sector are considered raw materials for other industries. Major businesses in this sector include agriculture, agribusiness, fishing, forestry and all mining and quarrying industries.
Capital market	A Capital market is a market for securities (both debt and equity), where business enterprises (companies) and governments can raise long-term funds. It is defined as a market in which money is lent for periods longer than a year, as the raising of short-term funds takes place on other markets (e.g., the money market). The Capital market includes the stock market (equity securities) and the bond market (debt).
Coordination failure	Coordination failure is the electoral problem resulting from competition between two or more candidates or political parties from the same or approximate location in the political ideological spectrum or space against an opposing candidate or political party from the other side of the political ideological spectrum or space. The resulting fragmentation of political support may result in electoral defeat. Coordination failures, and thus political calculations attempting to avoid them, appear most frequently in elections involving executives and representatives from single member districts.
Import	Balance of trade represents a difference in value f and export for a country. A country has demand for an Import when domestic quantity demanded exceeds domestic quantity supplied, or when the price of the good (or service) on the world market is less than the price on the domestic market. The balance of trade, usually denoted NX, is the difference between the value of the goods (and services) a country exports and the value of the goods the country Imports: $NX = X - I$, or equivalently $I = X - NX$ A trade deficit occurs when Imports are large relative to exports.
Income distribution	In economics, the Lorenz curve is a graphical representation of the cumulative distribution function of a probability distribution; it is a graph showing the proportion of the distribution assumed by the bottom y% of the values. It is often used to represent income Distribution, where it shows for the bottom x% of households, what percentage y% of the total income they have. The percentage of households is plotted on the x-axis, the percentage of income on the y-axis.

Import substitution industrialization	Import substitution industrialization is a trade and economic policy based on the premise that a country should attempt to reduce its foreign dependency through the local production of industrialized products. Adopted in many Latin American countries from the 1930s until the late 1980s, and in some Asian and African countries from the 1950s on, Import substitution industrialization was theoretically organized in the works of Raúl Prebisch, Hans Singer, Celso Furtado and other structural economic thinkers, and gained prominence with the creation of the United Nations Economic Commission for Latin America and the Caribbean . Insofar as its suggestion of state-induced industrialization through governmental spending, it is largely influenced by Keynesian thinking, as well as the infant industry arguments adopted by some highly industrialized countries, such as the United States, until the 1940s.
International Trade	International trade is exchange of capital, goods, and services across international borders or territories. In most countries, it represents a significant share of gross domestic product (GDP). While International trade has been present throughout much of history , its economic, social, and political importance has been on the rise in recent centuries.
Good	In macroeconomics and accounting, a good is contrasted with a service. In this sense, a good is defined as a physical (tangible) product, capable of being delivered to a purchaser and involves the transfer of ownership from seller to customer, say an apple, as opposed to an (intangible) service, say a haircut. A more general term that preserves the distinction between goods and services is "commodities," like a flashlight.
Choice Set	A Choice Set is one scenario, also known as a treatment, provided for evaluation by respondents in a Choice Experiment. Responses are collected and used to create a Choice Model. Respondents are usually provided with a series of differing Choice Sets for evaluation.
Price	price in economics and business is the result of an exchange and from that trade we assign a numerical monetary value to a good, service or asset. If Alice trades Bob 4 apples for an orange, the price of an orange is 4 apples. Inversely, the price of an apple is 1/4 oranges.
Supply and demand	Supply and demand is an economic model based on price, utility and quantity in a market. It concludes that in a competitive market, price will function to equalize the quantity demanded by consumers, and the quantity supplied by producers, resulting in an economic equilibrium of price and quantity.
	The demand schedule, depicted graphically as the demand curve, represents the amount of goods that buyers are willing and able to purchase at various prices, assuming all other non-price factors remain the same.
Elasticity	In economics, elasticity is the ratio of the percent change in one variable to the percent change in another variable. It is a tool for measuring the responsiveness of a function to changes in parameters in a relative way. Commonly analyzed are elasticity of substitution, price and wealth.
Exchange rate	Exchange rates Currency band Exchange rate Exchange rate regime Fixed Exchange rate Floating Exchange rate Linked Exchange rate

Markets
effective Exchange rate
· 5 Uncovered interest rate parity
· 6 Asset market model
· 7 Fluctuations in Exchange rates
· 8 .

Demand	In economics, demand is the desire to own anything and the ability to pay for it. . The term demand signifies the ability or the willingness to buy a particular commodity at a given point of time.
Demand curve	In economics, the Demand curve can be defined as the graph depicting the relationship between the price of a certain commodity, and the amount of it that consumers are willing and able to purchase at that given price. It is a graphic representation of a demand schedule. The Demand curve for all consumers together follows from the Demand curve of every individual consumer: the individual demands at each price are added together.
Information	Information as a concept has many meanings, from everyday usage to technical settings. The concept of Information is closely related to notions of constraint, communication, control, data, form, instruction, knowledge, meaning, mental stimulus, pattern, perception, and representation.

The English word was apparently derived from the Latin accusative form of the nominative (informatio): this noun is in its turn derived from the verb "informare" (to inform) in the sense of "to give form to the mind", "to discipline", "instruct", "teach": "Men so wise should go and inform their kings." (1330) Inform itself comes from the Latin verb informare, to give form to, to form an idea of. |
| Complete Information | Complete information is a term used in economics and game theory to describe an economic situation or game in which knowledge about other market participants or players is available to all participants. Every player knows the payoffs and strategies available to other players.

Complete information is one of the theoretical pre-conditions of an efficient perfectly competitive market. |
| Consumer | Consumer is a broad label that refers to any individuals or households that use goods and services generated within the economy. The concept of a Consumer is used in different contexts, so that the usage and significance of the term may vary.

Typically when business people and economists talk of Consumers they are talking about person as Consumer, an aggregated commodity item with little individuality other than that expressed in the buy/not-buy decision. |
| Consumer surplus | The term surplus is used in economics for several related quantities. The Consumer surplus is the amount that consumers benefit by being able to purchase a product for a price that is less than they would be willing to pay. The producer surplus is the amount that producers benefit by selling at a market price mechanism that is higher than they would be willing to sell for. |
| Returns to scale | In economics, Returns to scale and economies of scale are related terms that describe what happens as the scale of production increases. They are different terms and should not be used interchangeably. . |

Externality	In economics, an Externality or spillover of an economic transaction is an impact on a party that is not directly involved in the transaction. In such a case, prices do not reflect the full costs or benefits in production or consumption of a product or service. An advantageous impact is called an external benefit or positive Externality, while a detrimental impact is called an external cost or negative Externality.
Import quota	An Import quota is a type of protectionist trade restriction that sets a physical limit on the quantity of a good that can be imported into a country in a given period of time. Quotas, like other trade restrictions, are used to benefit the producers of a good in a domestic economy at the expense of all consumers of the good in that economy.
	Critics say quotas often lead to corruption (bribes to get a quota allocation), smuggling (circumventing a quota), and higher prices for consumers.
Export subsidy	Export subsidy is a government policy to encourage export of goods and discourage sale of goods on the domestic market through low-cost loans or tax relief for exporters government financed international advertising or R&D which means domestic consumers pay more than foreign consumers. The WTO prohibits most subsidies directly linked to the volume of exports.
	Export Subsidies are also generated when internal price supports as in a guaranteed minimum price for a commodity creates more production than can be consumed internally in the country.
Structural adjustment	Structural adjustment is a term used to describe the policy changes implemented by the International Monetary Fund (IMF) and the World Bank (the Bretton Woods Institutions) in developing countries. These policy changes are conditions (Conditionalities) for getting new loans from the IMF or World Bank, or for obtaining lower interest rates on existing loans. Conditionalities are implemented to ensure that the money lent will be spent in accordance with the overall goals of the loan.
Debt	debt is that which is owed; usually referencing assets owed, but the term can also cover moral obligations and other interactions not requiring money. In the case of assets, debt is a means of using future purchasing power in the present before a summation has been earned. Some companies and corporations use debt as a part of their overall corporate finance strategy.
Crisis	A Crisis may occur on a personal or societal level. It may be an unstable and dangerous social situation, in political, social, economic, military affairs, or a large-scale environmental event, especially one involving an impending abrupt change. More loosely, it is a term meaning "a testing time" or "emergency event".
Devaluation	Devaluation is a reduction in the value of a currency with respect to other monetary units. In common modern usage, it specifically implies an official lowering of the value of a country"s currency within a fixed exchange rate system, by which the monetary authority formally sets a new fixed rate with respect to a foreign reference currency. In contrast, depreciation is used for the unofficial decrease in the exchange rate in a floating exchange rate system.
Hyperinflation	Certain figures in this article use scientific notation for readability.
	In economics, Hyperinflation is inflation that is very high or "out of control", a condition in which prices increase rapidly as a currency loses its value. Definitions used by the media vary from a cumulative inflation rate over three years approaching 100% to "inflation exceeding 50% a month." In informal usage the term is often applied to much lower rates.

Depreciation	Composite life equals the total Depreciable Cost divided by the total Depreciation Per Year. $5,900 / $1,300 = 4.5 years. Composite Depreciation Rate equals Depreciation Per Year divided by total Historical Cost.
Balance of payments	In economics, the Balance of payments, measures the payments that flow between any individual country and all other countries. It is used to summarize all international economic transactions for that country during a specific time period, usually a year. The Balance of payments is determined by the country"s exports and imports of goods, services, and financial capital, as well as financial transfers.
Payment	A Payment is the transfer of wealth from one party (such as a person or company) to another. A Payment is usually made in exchange for the provision of goods, services or both, or to fulfill a legal obligation.
	The simplest and oldest form of Payment is barter, the exchange of one good or service for another.
Nominative determinism	Nominative determinism refers to the theory that a person"s name is given an influential role in reflecting key attributes of his job, profession, but real examples are more highly prized, the more obscure the better.
Privatization	Privatization is the incidence or process of transferring ownership of a business, enterprise, agency or public service from the public sector (government) to the private sector (business). In a broader sense, Privatization refers to transfer of any government function to the private sector including governmental functions like revenue collection and law enforcement.
	The term "Privatization" also has been used to describe two unrelated transactions.
Bank	The Bank or Company of Saint George (Italian: Ufficio di San Giorgio in Genoa or Casa di San Giorgio) was a financial institution of the Republic of Genoa. Founded in 1407, it was one of the oldest chartered Banks in Europe, if not the world. The Bank"s headquarters were at the Palazzo San Giorgio, which was built in the 13th century by order of Guglielmo Boccanegra, uncle of Simone Boccanegra, the first Doge of Genoa.
International Monetary Fund	The International Monetary Fund is an international organization that oversees the global financial system by following the macroeconomic policies of its member countries, in particular those with an impact on exchange rates and the balance of payments. It is an organization formed with a stated objective of stabilizing international exchange rates and facilitating development. It also offers highly leveraged loans mainly to poorer countries.
Dot-com bubble	The "Dot-com bubble" (or) was a speculative bubble covering roughly 1998-2001 (with a climax on March 10, 2000 with the NASDAQ peaking at 5132.52) during which stock markets in Western nations saw their equity value rise rapidly from growth in the more recent Internet sector and related fields. While the latter part was a boom and bust cycle, the Internet boom sometimes is meant to refer to the steady commercial growth of the Internet with the advent of the world wide web as exemplified by the first release of the Mosaic web browser in 1993 and continuing through the 1990s.
	The period was marked by the founding (and, in many cases, spectacular failure) of a group of new Internet-based companies commonly referred to as dot-coms.
Financial markets	In economics, a financial market is a mechanism that allows people to easily buy and sell (trade) financial securities (such as stocks and bonds), commodities (such as precious metals or agricultural goods), and other fungible items of value at low transaction costs and at prices that reflect the efficient-market hypothesis.
	Financial markets have evolved significantly over several hundred years and are undergoing constant innovation to improve liquidity.

Both general markets (where many commodities are traded) and specialized markets (where only one commodity is traded) exist.

Loan

A Loan is a type of debt. Like all debt instruments, a Loan entails the redistribution of financial assets over time, between the lender and the borrower.

In a Loan, the borrower initially receives or borrows an amount of money, called the principal, from the lender, and is obligated to pay back or repay an equal amount of money to the lender at a later time.

Nominative determinism	Nominative determinism refers to the theory that a person"s name is given an influential role in reflecting key attributes of his job, profession, but real examples are more highly prized, the more obscure the better.
Trade	Trade is the voluntary exchange of goods, services, or both. Trade is also called commerce or transaction. A mechanism that allows Trade is called a market.
Free Trade	Free trade is a type of trade policy that allows traders to act and transact without interference from government. According to the law of comparative advantage the policy permits trading partners mutual gains from trade of goods and services. Under a Free trade policy, prices are a reflection of true supply and demand, and are the sole determinant of resource allocation.
Coordination game	In game theory, Coordination games are a class of games with multiple pure strategy Nash equilibria in which players choose the same or corresponding strategies. Coordination games are a formalization of the idea of a coordination problem, which is widespread in the social sciences, including economics, meaning situations in which all parties can realize mutual gains, but only by making mutually consistent decisions. A common application is the choice of technological standards.
Trade pact	A trade pact is a wide ranging tax, tariff and trade pact that often includes investment guarantees. trade pacts are frequently politically contentious since they may change economic customs and deepen interdependence with trade partners. Increasing efficiency through "free trade" is a common goal.
Unilateralism	Unilateralism is any doctrine or agenda that supports one-sided action. Such action may be in disregard for other parties, or as an expression of a commitment toward a direction which other parties may find agreeable. Unilateralism is a neologism, (used in all countries) coined to be an antonym for multilateralism --the doctrine which asserts the benefits of participation from as many parties as possible.
Common Market	A common market is a type of trade bloc which is composed of a customs union with common policies on product regulation, and freedom of movement of the factors of production (capital and labour) and of enterprise. The goal is that the movement of capital, labour, goods, and services between the members is as easy as within them. This is the fourth stage of economic integration.
Anecdotal value	In economics, Anecdotal value refers to the primarily social and political value of an anecdote or anecdotal evidence in promoting understanding of a social, cultural, in the last several decades the evaluation of anecdotes has received sustained academic scrutiny from economists and scholars such as S.G. Checkland (on David Ricardo), Steven Novella, Hollis Robbins, R. Charleton, Kwamena Kwansah-Aidoo, and others; these academics seek to quantify the value inherent in the deployment of anecdotes. More recently, economists studying choice models have begun assessing Anecdotal value in the context of framing; Kahneman and Tversky suggest that choice models may be contingent on stories or anecdotes that frame or influence choice.
Free Trade Agreement	A Free trade agreement is a trade treaty between two or more countries. Usually these agreements are between two countries and are meant to reduce or completely remove tariffs to trade. According to the World Trade Organization there are more than 200 Free trade agreements in force.

North American Free Trade Agreement	The North American Free Trade Agreement is an agreement signed by the governments of the United States, Canada, and Mexico creating a trilateral trade bloc in North America. The agreement came into force on January 1, 1994. It superseded the Canada-United States Free Trade Agreement between the U.S. and Canada.
	In terms of combined purchasing power parity GDP of its members, as of 2007 the trade block is the largest in the world and second largest by nominal GDP comparison.
	The North American Free Trade Agreement has two supplements, the North American Agreement on Environmental Cooperation (NAAEC) and the North American Agreement on Labor Cooperation (NAALC).
Missing Market	A Missing market is a situation in microeconomics where a competitive market allowing the exchange of a commodity would be Pareto-efficient, but no such market exists.
	A variety of factors can lead to Missing markets:
	A classic example of a Missing market is the case of an externality like pollution, where decision makers are not responsible for some of the consequences of their actions. When a factory discharges polluted water into a river, that pollution can hurt people who fish in or get their drinking water from the river downstream, but the factory owner may have no incentive to consider those consequences.
Protectionism	Protectionism is the economic policy of restraining trade between states, through methods such as tariffs on imported goods, restrictive quotas, and a variety of other restrictive government regulations designed to discourage imports, and prevent foreign take-over of local markets and companies. This policy is closely aligned with anti-globalization, and contrasts with free trade, where government barriers to trade are kept to a minimum. The term is mostly used in the context of economics, where Protectionism refers to policies or doctrines which "protect" businesses and workers within a country by restricting or regulating trade with foreign nations.
Import	
	Balance of trade represents a difference in value f and export for a country. A country has demand for an Import when domestic quantity demanded exceeds domestic quantity supplied, or when the price of the good (or service) on the world market is less than the price on the domestic market.
	The balance of trade, usually denoted NX, is the difference between the value of the goods (and services) a country exports and the value of the goods the country Imports:
	$NX = X - I$, or equivalently $I = X - NX$
	A trade deficit occurs when Imports are large relative to exports.
Trade barrier	A Trade barrier is a general term that describes any government policy or regulation that restricts international trade. The barriers can take many forms, including the following terms that include many restrictions in international trade within multiple countries that import and export any items of trade.

· Import duty
· Import licenses
· Export licenses
· Import quotas
· Tariffs
· Subsidies
· Non-tariff barriers to trade
· Voluntary Export Restraints
· Local Content Requirements
· Embargo

Most Trade barriers work on the same principle: the imposition of some sort of cost on trade that raises the price of the traded products. If two or more nations repeatedly use Trade barriers against each other, then a trade war results.

Multilateralism

multilateralism is a term in international relations that refers to multiple countries working in concert on a given issue.

Most international organizations, such as the United Nations (UN) and the World Trade Organization are multilateral in nature. The main proponents of multilateralism have traditionally been the middle powers such as Canada, Australia, Switzerland, the Benelux countries and the Nordic countries.

Trade creation

Trade creation is an economic term related to international economics in which trade is created by the formation of a customs union.

When a customs union is formed, the member nations establish a free trade area amongst themselves and a common external tariff on non-member nations. As a result, the member nations establish greater trading ties between themselves now that protectionist barriers such as tariffs, quotas, and non-tariff barriers such as subsidies have been eliminated.

Trade diversion

Trade diversion is an economic term related to international economics in which trade is diverted from a more efficient exporter towards a less efficient one by the formation of a free trade agreement.

When a country applies the same tariff to all nations, it will always import from the most efficient producer, since the more efficient nation will provide the goods at a lower price. With the establishment of a bilateral or regional free trade agreement, that may not be the case.

Change

changes can refer to:

· A jazz term for chord progression

· changes (band), an American folk band
· The changes (band), an American rock band

· changes (The Monkees album), The Monkees" ninth studio album
· changes, Christopher Wiliams" second studio album
· changes, an album by R. Carlos Nakai
· changes (Taylor Horn album), Taylor Horn"s third studio album
· changesbowie, a David Bowie compilation album
· changes (Kelly Osbourne album), Kelly Osbourne"s second studio album
· changes (Vanilla Sky album), Vanilla Sky"s third album
· changes (Jarrett album), by Keith Jarrett, Jack DeJohnette and Gary Peacock
· changes (Billy "Crash" Craddock album)
· changes (Lisa Miskovsky album)
· changes (Tanya Tucker album)
· changes, an album by Johnny Rivers

· "changes" (David Bowie song), a song by David Bowie on his 1971 album Hunky Dory
· "changes" (2Pac song), a song by Tupac Shakur on his Greatest Hits album
· "changes" (Black Sabbath song), a ballad by Black Sabbath, remade as a duet by Kelly and Ozzy Osbourne
· "changes" (Will Young song), a song by Will Young on his fourth studio album, Let It Go
· "changes" (Gareth Gates song), a song by Gareth Gates, from the album Pictures of the Other Side
· "changes" (Imagination song), a song by Imagination, from the album In the Heat of the Night
· "changes", a song by Yes on the album 90125
· "changes", a song by "Buddy" Miles ' Jimi Hendrix on the album Band of Gypsys
· "changes", a song by Jane"s Addiction
· "changes", a song by Phil Ochs
· "changes", a song by Godsmack on the album Faceless
· "changes", a song by The Zombies on the album Odessey and Oracle
· "changes", a song by 3 Doors Down on the album Away from the Sun
· "changes", a song by Sugar on the album Copper Blue
· "changes", a song by Chris Lake
· "changes", a song by Moby Grape on their album Moby Grape
· "changes", a song by Santana on their album Zebop!

· The changes (TV series), produced by the BBC in 1975. Also the changes Trilogy of novels on which the series was based, written by Peter Dickinson .

Heckscher-Ohlin model	The Heckscher-Ohlin model (H-O model) is a general equilibrium mathematical model of international trade, developed by Eli Heckscher and Bertil Ohlin at the Stockholm School of Economics. It builds on David Ricardo"s theory of comparative advantage by predicting patterns of commerce and production based on the factor endowments of a trading region. The model essentially says that countries will export products that utilize their abundant and cheap factor(s) of production and import products that utilize the countries" scarce factor(s).

Organisation for Economic Co-operation and Development	The Organisation for Economic Co-operation and Development (OECD) is an international organisation of 30 countries that accept the principles of representative democracy and free-market economy. Most OECD members are high-income economies with a high HDI and are regarded as developed countries. It originated in 1948 as the Organisation for European Economic Co-operation , led by Robert Marjolin of France, to help administer the Marshall Plan for the reconstruction of Europe after World War II. Later, its membership was extended to non-European states.
Unemployment	Unemployment occurs when a person is available to work and seeking work but currently without work. The prevalence of Unemployment is usually measured using the Unemployment rate, which is defined as the percentage of those in the labor force who are unemployed. The Unemployment rate is also used in economic studies and economic indices such as the United States" Conference Board"s Index of Leading Indicators as a measure of the state of the macroeconomics.
Wage	Several countries have enacted a statutory minimum Wage rate that sets a price floor for certain kinds of labor. Wage derives from words which suggest "making a promise," often in monetary form. Specifically from the Old French word wagier or gagier meaning to pledge or promise, from which the money placed in a bet also derives.
Import substitution industrialization	Import substitution industrialization is a trade and economic policy based on the premise that a country should attempt to reduce its foreign dependency through the local production of industrialized products. Adopted in many Latin American countries from the 1930s until the late 1980s, and in some Asian and African countries from the 1950s on, Import substitution industrialization was theoretically organized in the works of Raúl Prebisch, Hans Singer, Celso Furtado and other structural economic thinkers, and gained prominence with the creation of the United Nations Economic Commission for Latin America and the Caribbean . Insofar as its suggestion of state-induced industrialization through governmental spending, it is largely influenced by Keynesian thinking, as well as the infant industry arguments adopted by some highly industrialized countries, such as the United States, until the 1940s.
Andean Pact	The Andean Community is a trade bloc comprising the South American countries of Bolivia, Colombia, Ecuador and Peru. The trade bloc was called the Andean Pact until 1996 and came into existence with the signing of the Cartagena Agreement in 1969. Its headquarters are located in Lima, Peru. The Andean Community has 98 million inhabitants living in an area of 4,700,000 square kilometers, whose Gross Domestic Product amounted to US$745.3 billion in 2005, including Venezuela, (who was a member at that time).
Africa	Africa has a large quantity of natural resources including oil, diamonds, gold, cobalt, uranium, copper, bauxite, but also woods and tropical fruits. Having a low human density, for a long period of time Africa has been colonized by more dynamic groups, exploiting African resources. Some economists have talked about the "scurge of raw materials", large quantities of rare raw materials putting Africa under heavy pressures and tensions, leading to wars and slow development.

Game theory	The games studied in Game theory are well-defined mathematical objects. A game consists of a set of players, a set of moves (or strategies) available to those players, and a specification of payoffs for each combination of strategies. Most cooperative games are presented in the characteristic function form, while the extensive and the normal forms are used to define noncooperative games.
Nash equilibrium	In game theory, Nash equilibrium is a solution concept of a game involving two or more players, in which each player is assumed to know the equilibrium strategies of the other players, and no player has anything to gain by changing only his or her own strategy unilaterally. If each player has chosen a strategy and no player can benefit by changing his or her strategy while the other players keep theirs unchanged, then the current set of strategy choices and the corresponding payoffs constitute a Nash equilibrium.
	Stated simply, Amy and Bill are in Nash equilibrium if Amy is making the best decision she can, taking into account Bill"s decision, and Bill is making the best decision he can, taking into account Amy"s decision.
Industry	An industry is the manufacturing of a good or service within a category. Although industry is a broad term for any kind of economic production, in economics and urban planning industry is a synonym for the secondary sector, which is a type of economic activity involved in the manufacturing of raw materials into goods and products.
	There are four key industrial economic sectors: the primary sector, largely raw material extraction industries such as mining and farming; the secondary sector, involving refining, construction, and manufacturing; the tertiary sector, which deals with services and distribution of manufactured goods; and the quaternary sector, a relatively new type of knowledge industry focusing on technological research, design and development such as computer programming, and biochemistry.
Principal-agent problem	In political science and economics, the Principal-agent problem or agency dilemma treats the difficulties that arise under conditions of incomplete and asymmetric information when a principal hires an agent, such as the problem that the two may not have the same interests, while the principal is, presumably, hiring the agent to pursue the interests of the former.
	Various mechanisms may be used to try to align the interests of the agent in solidarity with those of the principal, such as piece rates/commissions, profit sharing, efficiency wages, performance measurement (including financial statements), the agent posting a bond, or fear of firing. The Principal-agent problem is found in most employer/employee relationships, for example, when stockholders hire top executives of corporations.
Repeated game	In game theory, a Repeated game (or iterated game) is an extensive form game which consists in some number of repetitions of some base game (called a stage game). The stage game is usually one of the well-studied 2-person games. It captures the idea that a player will have to take into account the impact of his current action on the future actions of other players; this is sometimes called his reputation.
Time horizon	A Time horizon, also known as a planning horizon, is a fixed point of time in the future at which point certain processes will be evaluated or assumed to end. It is necessary in an accounting, finance or risk management regime to assign such a fixed horizon time so that alternatives can be evaluated for performance over the same period of time. A Time horizon is a physical impossibility in the real world.

Cross-sectional data	Cross-sectional data or cross section (of a study population) in statistics and econometrics is a type of one-dimensional data set. Cross-sectional data refers to data collected by observing many subjects (such as individuals, firms or countries/regions) at the same point of time, or without regard to differences in time. Analysis of Cross-sectional data usually consists of comparing the differences among the subjects.
Mean	In statistics, mean has two related meanings: · the arithmetic mean . · the expected value of a random variable, which is also called the population mean. It is sometimes stated that the "mean" means average. This is incorrect if "mean" is taken in the specific sense of "arithmetic mean" as there are different types of averages: the mean, median, and mode.
Regression analysis	In statistics, Regression analysis includes any techniques for modeling and analyzing several variables, when the focus is on the relationship between a dependent variable and one or more independent variables. More specifically, Regression analysis helps us understand how the typical value of the dependent variable changes when any one of the independent variables is varied, while the other independent variables are held fixed. Most commonly, Regression analysis estimates the conditional expectation of the dependent variable given the independent variables -- that is, the average value of the dependent variable when the independent variables are held fixed.
Time series	In statistics, signal processing, and many other fields, a Time series is a sequence of data points, measured typically at successive times, spaced at (often uniform) time intervals. Time series analysis comprises methods that attempt to understand such Time series, often either to understand the underlying context of the data points (Where did they come from? What generated them?), or to make forecasts (predictions). Time series forecasting is the use of a model to forecast future events based on known past events: to forecast future data points before they are measured.
Standard deviation	In probability theory and statistics, the Standard deviation of a statistical population, a data set or a probability distribution is the square root of its being algebraically more tractable though practically less robust than the expected deviation or average absolute deviation. A low Standard deviation indicates that the data points tend to be very close to the mean, whereas high Standard deviation indicates that the data are spread out over a large range of values.
Correlation	In statistics, Correlation (often measured as a Correlation coefficient, ρ) indicates the strength and direction of a linear relationship between two random variables. That is in contrast with the usage of the term in colloquial speech, which denotes any relationship, not necessarily linear. In general statistical usage, Correlation or co-relation refers to the departure of two random variables from independence.
Covariance	In probability theory and statistics, covariance is a measure of how much two variables change together. (Variance is a special case of the covariance when the two variables are identical). The covariance between two real-valued random variables X and Y, with expected values $E(X) = \mu$ and $E(Y) = \nu$ is defined as $$\mathrm{Cov}(X, Y) = \mathrm{E}((X - \mu)(Y - \nu)),$$ where E is the expected value operator.

Random variables	In mathematics, random variables are used in the study of probability. They were developed to assist in the analysis of games of chance, stochastic events, and the results of scientific experiments by capturing only the mathematical properties necessary to answer probabilistic questions. Further formalizations have firmly grounded the entity in the theoretical domains of mathematics by making use of measure theory.
Scatter plot	A scatter plot is a type of mathematical diagram using Cartesian coordinates to display values for two variables for a set of data.
	The data is displayed as a collection of points, each having the value of one variable determining the position on the horizontal axis and the value of the other variable determining the position on the vertical axis. A scatter plot is also called a scatter chart, scatter diagram and scatter graph.
Ordinary least squares	In statistics and econometrics, ordinary least squares is a technique for estimating the unknown parameters in a linear regression model. This method minimizes the sum of squared distances between the observed responses in a set of data, and the fitted responses from the regression model. The linear least squares computational technique provides simple expressions for the estimated parameters in an ordinary least squares analysis, and hence for associated statistical values such as the standard errors of the parameters.
Multivariate statistics	Multivariate statistics is a form of statistics encompassing the simultaneous observation and analysis of more than one statistical variable. The application of Multivariate statistics is multivariate analysis. Methods of bivariate statistics, for example ANOVA and t-tests, are special cases of Multivariate statistics in which two variables are involved.
	There are many different models, each with its own type of analysis:
	· Clustering systems assign objects into groups (called clusters) so that objects from the same cluster are more similar to each other than objects from different clusters. · Hotelling"s T-square is a generalization of Student"s t statistic that is used in multivariate hypothesis testing. · Multivariate analysis of variance (MANOVA) methods extend analysis of variance methods to cover cases where there is more than one dependent variable and where the dependent variables cannot simply be combined. · Discriminant function or canonical variate analysis attempt to establish whether a set of variables can be used to distinguish between two or more groups. · Regression analysis attempts to determine a linear formula that can describe how some variables respond to changes in others.
Nonlinear	In mathematics, a nonlinear system is a system which is not linear, that is, a system which does not satisfy the superposition principle, a nonlinear system is any problem where the variable(s) to be solved for cannot be written as a linear combination of independent components. A nonhomogeneous system, which is linear apart from the presence of a function of the independent variables, is nonlinear according to a strict definition, but such systems are usually studied alongside linear systems, because they can be transformed to a linear system of multiple variables.
Alternative hypothesis	In statistical hypothesis testing, the Alternative hypothesis (or maintained hypothesis or research hypothesis) and the null hypothesis are the two rival hypotheses which are compared by a statistical hypothesis test. An example might be where water quality in a stream has been observed over many years and a test is made of the null hypothesis that there is no change in quality between the first and second halves of the data against the Alternative hypothesis that the quality is poorer in the second half of the record.

The concept of an Alternative hypothesis in testing was devised by Jerzy Neyman and Egon Pearson, and it is used in the Neyman-Pearson lemma.

Null hypothesis

In statistical hypothesis testing, the Null hypothesis (H_0) formally describes some aspect of the statistical "behaviour" of a set of data. This description is assumed to be valid unless the actual behaviour of the data contradicts this assumption. Thus, the Null hypothesis is contrasted against another or alternative hypothesis.

Standard error

The standard error of a method of measurement or estimation is the standard deviation of the sampling distribution associated with the estimation method. The term may also be used to refer to an estimate of that standard deviation, derived from a particular sample used to compute the estimate.

For example, the sample mean is the usual estimator of a population mean.

Hypothesis testing

A statistical hypothesis test is a method of making statistical decisions using experimental data. In statistics, a result is called statistically significant if it is unlikely to have occurred by chance. The phrase "test of significance" was coined by Ronald Fisher: "Critical tests of this kind may be called tests of significance, and when such tests are available we may discover whether a second sample is or is not significantly different from the first."

hypothesis testing is sometimes called confirmatory data analysis, in contrast to exploratory data analysis.

T-distribution

In probability and statistics, Student"s t-distribution (or simply the t-distribution) is a probability distribution that arises in the problem of estimating the mean of a normally distributed population when the sample size is small. It is the basis of the popular Student"s t-tests for the statistical significance of the difference between two sample means, and for confidence intervals for the difference between two population means. The Student"s t-distribution is a special case of the generalised hyperbolic distribution.

Confidence interval

In statistics, a Confidence interval is a particular kind of interval estimate of a population parameter. Instead of estimating the parameter by a single value, an interval likely to include the parameter is given. Thus, Confidence intervals are used to indicate the reliability of an estimate.